KT-872-077

THE FAME GAME

BEFORE WE BEGIN

Who would want to be an Olympic athlete? Just think about it: hours of hard training every day, having to get up early, to eat the right food, to go to bed when your friends are out having fun. And all for what? Just to run a little faster or jump a little higher (or whatever your sport is) than anyone else! Why would anybody put themselves through it ..?

GRUNT, GASP, SHUDDER

VICTORY!

The modern Olympic Games started in 1896, but they're based on the Olympic Games of the Ancient Greeks, which started in 796 BC and were held every four years without a break for more than a thousand years.

New sports at Atlanta, USA in 1996 included Mountain Biking, Beach Volleyball and Women's Football.

2,500 million people watched parts of the 1984 Los Angeles Games on television.

At Atlanta in 1996, $456 million was paid for the USA television rights alone.

CONTENTS

Watch out for the *Sign of the Foot*! Whenever you see this sign in the book it means there are some more details at the *FOOT* of the page. Like here.

What they don't tell you about

THE OLYMPICS

Loan:
retur
Libr
will
PLE

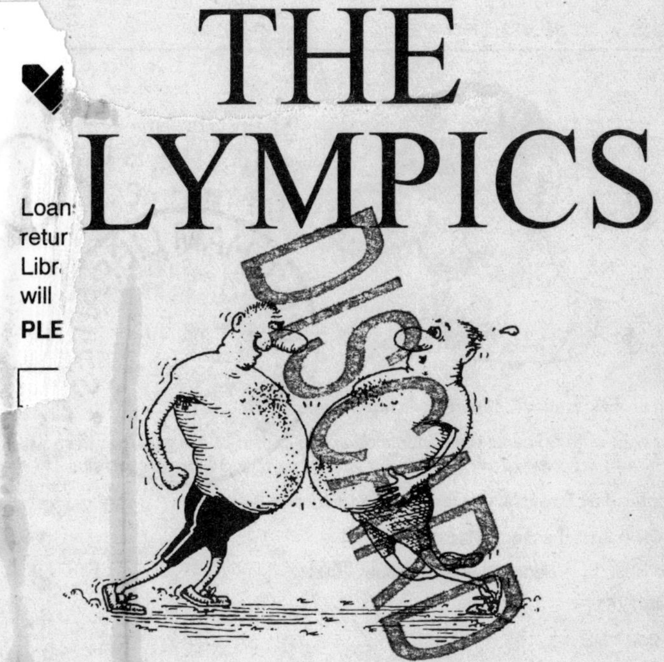

By Bob Fowke

Dedicated to belly-barging.
It's not an Olympic sport - but perhaps it should be.

a division of Hodder Headline Limited

Hello, I'm *Arfa Second*. Just for the *record*, I'm a runner and I'm fast. Come with me and we'll whip through the story of the Olympics faster than a pack of greyhounds after their favourite dog biscuit - and if you want to be an athlete you may find a few tips to chew on along the way.

TOWER HILL LIBRARY
Tower Hill B42 1LG
Tel: 0121 464 1948
BIRMINGHAM LIBRARIES
J796.48

Text and illustrations, copyright © Bob Fowke 2000

The right of Bob Fowke to be identified as the author of the work has been asserted by him in accordance with the Copyright, Designs and Patents Act 1988.

Produced by Fowke & Co. for Hodder Children's Books

Cover photo: the Stock Market

Published by Hodder Children's Books 2000

0340 736119

10 9 8 7 6 5 4 3

All rights reserved. No part of this publication may be reproduced, stored in a retrieval system, or transmitted, in any form or by any means, without the prior written permission of the publisher, nor be otherwise circulated in any form of binding or cover other than that in which it is published and without a similar condition being imposed on the subsequent purchaser.

Hodder Children's Books
A division of Hodder Headline Limited
338 Euston Road
London NW1 3BH

Printed and bound by The Guernsey Press Co. Ltd., Channel Islands
A catalogue record for this book is available from the British Library

The modern Olympics are the greatest sporting occasion in the world, and the reason athletes want to compete in them is the same now as it was nearly three thousand years ago: if they win gold at the Olympics then they know they're the best there is.

For athletes, there's nothing else like it.

It's Sydney, Sidney

This is Sidney, he's a skeet shooter. He's hoping to compete in the next Olympic Games, due in the year 2000. They're going to be held in - Sydney! That's Sydney Australia. The Australians are hoping that their Olympics will be the biggest and best ever:

- Nearly 10,000 competitors are expected at the Sydney Games.

- Seating for 728,000 spectators will be available at twenty-eight different sites including the main stadium, which alone will have seating for 110,000 people - the largest ever Olympic stadium.

- The Olympic Village will house 15,300 athletes and Olympic officials. In fact it's more of an Olympic Town, with 600 permanent buildings and 500 temporary homes. It will be the world's largest solar-powered suburb.

- The Sydney Games are expected to cost 2.6 billion Australian dollars (slightly under seven hundred million pounds at the time of writing).

Skeet shooting is an event at the Olympics.

Pierre's passion

The first modern Olympic Games were held in Athens in 1896. They were set up by Baron Pierre de Coubertin, a French aristocrat who thought that the young Frenchmen of his day were feeble and that that was why France kept losing wars. De Coubertin believed that the Olympic Games would encourage his fellow countrymen to get fit and be better able to defend their country.

Since 1896, there have been twenty-three Olympic Games, plus the extra 'Intercalated Games' (see page 43). During that time only three have been missed, all of them because of the two World Wars. The three missing Games were: Berlin 1916, Tokyo 1940 and London 1944. Except for those three missed Games, the Olympics have grown like a camel in a cake shop (assuming camels like cakes) ever since de Coubertin started them. In 1896 just 311 athletes from 13 nations competed. This had risen to more than 10,000 athletes from more than 196 nations at the last games in Atlanta, in 1996.

Greasy Greeks

The ancient Olympic Games were a festival of sport held at Olympia in Greece from at least 776 BC until AD 393. In actual fact, these ancient Games were as much about religion as they were about sport. They were held in praise of the gods: 'The gods are friends of the Games' as one Greek writer put it. The athletes competed naked and rubbed oil on their bodies before competing.

The ancient Olympics were held in the high heat of summer before a huge crowd of spectators who camped out under the stars until the festival was over. It may seem a long way from those ancient Olympics to the modern Games in their ultra-modern stadiums but, if we forget about the gods and the nudity, much of the spirit of the ancient Games is still with us today. Even our word 'athlete' comes from an ancient Greek word: it's based on the name of *Aethlius* who was a king of Elis, a region near Olympia.

BARE BEGINNINGS

GREASY GREEKS GET STARTED

TIME FOR A FESTIVAL

Ancient Greece was a jumble of tiny states, each one centered around a city. These 'city-states' were always quarrelling and then making up. However, despite being divided up like this and despite wars and quarrels, all Greeks felt that they belonged to the same family, the *Hellenes* which means 'Greeks'. They called everyone else *barbarians*.

The family of Ancient Greeks was bound together by language and religion and by three big *pan-hellenic* festivals: the *Panathenaea* held at Athens, a festival at Delphi, and the festival at Olympia. Athletic games were a major part of all three festivals, but especially at Olympia. Athletes and competitors from all over the Greek world would gather for the 'Olympic Games'.

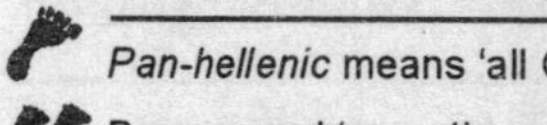

Pan-hellenic means 'all Greek'.

Pronounced 'pan-athen-eeya'.

Tailtean Games

Our word 'athlete' may come from the Ancient Greek, but that doesn't mean that the Ancient Greeks invented athletics, which are probably as old as the human race. The oldest known athletic festival is the *Lugnasard* or *Tailtean Games* which are said to have been held in Ireland as long ago as 1829 BC. Events at the games included jumping, javelin and hammer-throwing.

The games were founded by a chief called *Lugh of the Long Arm*, who was father of the famous Irish hero, Cuchulain (more on him later). Lugh called his games after his foster mother, *Tailti*.

Truce! Truce!

The ancient Olympics took place every four years in August or September at the time of the second full moon after the summer solstice  - but in daylight of course. Several weeks before the big day sacred *truce-bearers* would set out from Elis, a city near to Olympia which controlled the games. The truce-bearers wore crowns of laurel and each carried a staff. Their duty was to declare the start of a sacred truce stopping all wars throughout all the lands controlled

---

The day in mid-summer when the sun at midday is at its highest.

by Greeks, so that athletes and spectators could travel to Olympia in safety. Without a truce this would often have been impossible, seeing as Greeks were always fighting each other. To make sure that no one broke the truce, all athletes and spectators were said to be under the protection of *Zeus*, top god of the Greeks and god of the games.

The athletes trained together for at least a month in Elis, where they were kept in order by officials called *hellenodikai*, and by assistants known as *whip-bearers* whose job was to beat the athletes if they misbehaved. Their training finished a couple of days before the Olympic Games were due to begin, then the whole caboodle of athletes and officials set off for Olympia. It took the procession two full days to get there travelling on foot.

Hello campers!

Meanwhile at Olympia, the crowds were gathering. Apart from one building for important visitors, there was nowhere to stay so everyone camped out under the stars or in tents. August and September are hot in Greece so sleeping outside was no problem, but imagine a crowd of more than twenty thousand campers, with food stalls, entertainers and other hangers-on like a giant fair, in the heat of summer - and almost no drains! The stink must have been appalling. No wonder men prayed to *Zeus Apomyios*, 'Zeus who keeps flies away'! It wasn't until *nine hundred years* after the games had first been held that a rich Greek called Herodes paid for proper facilities to be built.

TIME TO PLAY!

In fact it's amazing that the Games remained as popular as they did. Apart from the stink, out of respect for Zeus no one was allowed to wear a hat. Death from sunstroke, such as that of the famous philosopher Thales in 546 BC, must have been quite common. In one Greek story a gentleman threatens to send his lazy slave to the Olympics as a punishment!

Nevertheless, the show was spectacular. The starting gates at the *Hippodrome* were 130 metres wide, big enough for up to forty four-horse chariots to line up behind them. In the centre was a statue of an eagle. The race started when a lever was pulled causing the eagle to rise in the air and a statue of a dolphin at the top of the gates to drop.

My Olympic Diary - by Glaucon the Greek

DAY 1: no sport today, watched the 'signing in' of the competitors who swore not to cheat. The judges decided who would compete in the boys' events and who would compete in the adults' events. That weirdo Pythagoras with his long hair and purple robes was not allowed to enter the boys' boxing because he looked like a weakling. Quite right too!

DAY 2: horse and chariot races in the morning at the *hippodrome*, then over to the stadium for the pentathlon (foot-race, long jump, discus, javelin and wrestling). Big feast in the evening given by a rich visitor.

Chariot racing was a very ancient sport. A chariot race in the early Greek poem, the *Odyssey*, by the poet Homer, describes how chariots raced over mud made slippery with the blood of sacrificial victims and how the hero Ajax slipped in the blood.

Something on Ancient Greek women's events shortly.

Pythagoras became a famous philosopher and mathematician.

DAY 3: a hundred oxen sacrificed this morning and their thighs burned on the altar to Zeus. Boys' events in the afternoon. The boxing was great, really tough - Pythagoras wouldn't have stood a chance.

DAY 3 continued: the high point of the festival today - the sacrifice to Zeus on the great altar near his temple, which always takes place on the morning after the full moon. The altar is made of the ashes of sacrificial victims mixed with water and kneaded into a paste [footnote].

DAY 4: athletics all day. Somehow young Pythagoras got himself accepted for the men's boxing - and won it! I always said he was a champion.

DAY 5: feasting all day, too much wine. I'll be going home with a headache!

[footnote] There was a sacrifice every day of the year on this altar. It grew to over seven metres tall.

GIRLS' GAMES

No women, slaves or foreigners were allowed to compete in the Olympics and women weren't allowed to watch either, except for one priestess. Women who sneaked in were thrown to their deaths from a cliff. Only one woman is known to have got away with it. *Pherenice* wanted to watch her son boxing and went to the Games disguised as his trainer. However, when he won she got so excited that she leapt over the barrier and it was obvious to everyone that she was a woman. She was let off because both her son and her husband were Olympic champions. From that day the athletes *and* trainers had to go naked, just to make sure!

Women had their own games controlled by women, where men weren't allowed except for a few officials. They were called the *Heraea* (footprint) and were dedicated to the goddess Hera, the sister and wife of Zeus. The girls ran races just like the boys, but five-sixths of the distance. Unlike the boys they wore a short tunic. (In the city-state of Sparta the girls ran naked as well.) Some Greeks thought that the Heraea came first and the Olympic Games were originally copied from them, especially since a temple to Hera was the oldest building at Olympia.

Winners wore a crown of olive leaves and got a share of cows sacrificed to Hera to eat.

(footprint) Pronounced 'heh-ree-a'.

Oil and dust

Before competing, ancient athletes (men and women) would rub their bodies with oil (the wrestlers then had to dust themselves so as to give a good grip to their opponents) and from around 720 BC all competed *gymnos* or naked, which is where we get the words 'gymnastics' and 'gymnasium' (gym) from. They trained hard but maybe Greek writers exaggerated what their athletes could do. One runner is said to have been able to outpace hares and another was said to have raced a horse. There were the same sort of stories about wrestlers and weight-lifters.

Other Greek games not included in the Olympics included kissing competitions and trying to stand on a greasy wine skin for as long as possible.

I WIN – AND YOU LOSE

In the book *Alice in Wonderland* by Lewis Carroll a dodo at a croquet game says: 'everybody has won, and all must have prizes'. Such an idea was the exact opposite of everything the Ancient Greeks believed in. They played to *win* - there were no second or third prizes among the Ancient Greeks. The athletes hated losing so much that they used to pray for 'death or the wreath' (the wreath was their version of a gold medal). They never spoke of their competitions as 'games', always calling them 'contests' or *agon* - which we get our word 'agony' from.

What they admired was *victory*. Victors were happy and proud, they could afford to be kind to losers - if the losers waited around. Victors had *aidos*, a quality of calm, unboastful superiority which meant that they were blessed by the gods. Losers just slunk away in disgrace.

The *dodo* is an extinct bird.

Feelings often ran high and certainly not everyone had *aidos*. One boxer was so angry at being kept out of a competition due to late arrival that he punched the victor during the award ceremony. Awards included draping the victor in a length of wool a bit like a scarf and crowning him with a wreath of wild olive leaves, which had been cut by a boy with a golden sickle. The olive trees where the wreaths came from were said to have been planted by a hero called Herakles.

THE END IS NIGH!

Greece was conquered by the Romans in around 190 BC. The ancient Games continued under Roman rule, although they were never as important again. The Romans looked down on athletics, even though the Roman general Sulla tried to move the Games to Rome - as if the sacred Games of Zeus could just be carted from place to place like a circus!

Even Romans who liked athletics tended to do more harm than good: the Emperor Nero drove a ten horse chariot in the chariot race but fell off because he was drunk. He won the prize anyway: there were no other competitors - only a madman would race against a

Roman emperor. It was at this time that Nero removed the statues of previous victors from Olympia and had them thrown in the sewers.

A far greater danger then loomed: a new religion called Christianity had begun to spread across the Roman Empire. The Olympics were a festival in honour of the god Zeus, and Christians didn't like people to worship any god other than their own. They tried several times to stop the Games, and they were finally abolished by the Christian Emperor Theodosius I in AD 393.

 Some scholars disagree with this date.

Let's Start Again

Game plans in preparation

More than a thousand years later ...

For more than a thousand years Olympia lay abandoned: the statue of Zeus was destroyed, the buildings crumbled, grass covered the tracks in the stadium.

When in 1766 an English scholar called Richard Chandler 'discovered' the site while on a tour of Greece , there was almost nothing left to show what Olympia had once been.

The local Greeks have always scoffed at his 'discovery', claiming that they knew all along what the ruins were.

Greece was a long way away from Western Europe and it was ruled by the Turks at that time. There was no way to investigate the site further. Two years later, a German historian called Winkelman who tried to follow up on Chandler's discovery was murdered by bandits before he could even get there.

It wasn't until 1875 that Ernst Curtius, another German professor, was able to begin excavations.

Meantime the story of the modern Olympics moved to France, where, at the Battle of Sedan in 1870, the French Emperor Napoleon III had been captured by the Germans along with most of the French army, causing France to lose the Franco-Prussian War.

French nobleman, Baron Pierre de Coubertin, was a child at the time of Sedan. He grew up in the shadow of that terrible defeat but also at a time when Curtius's discoveries at Olympia were being talked about all over Europe, awakening interest in all things Olympic.

De Coubertin came to believe that the reason France had lost at Sedan was because the French soldiers had been too unfit and feeble to fight properly. He decided that an international festival of athletics modelled on the ancient Olympics would be just the thing to encourage his fellow countrymen to get fit.

De Coubertin admired the British and he especially admired the British love of sport. Above all he worshipped *Thomas Arnold*. Arnold had been headmaster of Rugby School from 1828 to 1842 where he had encouraged sport as part of school life. During a tour of England in 1886, de Coubertin had a vision while standing beside Arnold's tomb in the Rugby School chapel. It was this vision that finally decided de Coubertin on his life's work. He decided to restart the Olympic Games.

Made in Britain

As de Coubertin saw, nineteenth century Britain was mad about sport of all kinds. In fact sport in its modern form is one of the major British contributions to the rest of the world, along with the English language and the Industrial Revolution. The very word 'sport' comes from the old English *disport* - to enjoy oneself. And like sport itself the word has spread round the world.

British background

British interest in sport started long ago. The earliest definite description of an English athlete is of Saint Cuthbert (*c.* AD 634-87) who was good at running, jumping and wrestling.

By the time of Henry II (1133-89) open spaces outside London were being set aside for young Londoners to practise. Kings themselves joined in - Henry V (1387-1422) was such a fast runner that with two of his lords he could run down a deer and capture it barehanded.

WAKE UP!

Before the nineteenth century, the main British sporting competitions took place at wakes and fairs, wild festivals where all ages and sexes took part. A common prize for the girls was a smock or shirt, often called a *she-shirt*, and for the boys it was a hat. As well as running, wrestling, boxing and jumping, other events were dreamt up which are less common now at major athletics meetings:

Wakes were ancient festivals, held to commemorate the founding of churches. They usually took place in churchyards.

The madness mounts

Apart from a period in the seventeenth century when prim *puritans* put a stop to all wakes and fairs, sport-fever tightened its grip on Britain as time went by. It was almost a madness: during the eighteenth century fortunes were won and lost on bets on all kinds of sporting competitions - as well as on such 'sports' as cock-fighting and dog-fighting. Favourites were bare-knuckle boxing, and walking and running races.

The madness took firmest hold among schoolboys, and by the nineteenth century sport-fever had infected all the English public schools. A keen cricketer at Eton could play at least *twenty-one hours* of cricket per week.

Public schools were for the well-off, but they weren't quite the posh places they are today. They were rough and very tough and the boys often fought back against their masters as well as against each other - to such an extent that there were violent rebellions at all the major schools. At Winchester and Rugby the local militia had to be called out to restore order.

Puritans were a type of strict Christian who wanted to 'purify' the Church of England (and Britain in general) of what they thought was un-Christian behaviour. They tried to put a stop to dancing, theatre and maypoles as well as sport.

It was the sport at English public schools which impressed Pierre de Coubertin. The tough hurly-burly was the opposite of French schooling which he blamed for the French defeat at Sedan. A best-selling book about Rugby School called *Tom Brown's Schooldays*, which came out in 1857, was his favourite book throughout his life (it's still a very good read). De Coubertin never really understood that his hero, the headmaster Thomas Arnold, only encouraged sport at Rugby because he wanted to tame his unruly, sport-mad pupils - without having to call out the militia!

Be that as it may, Rugby School held the first of its regular athletics meetings in 1856, and this was soon followed by meetings between other schools: Westminster played Charterhouse in 1861 and in 1864 Oxford University met Cambridge University. It was British schools and universities which gave sport its first rules and its modern form.

GRACEFULLY DONE!

When the British boys left school and university they naturally wanted to continue with their passion for sport. The first athletics club in the world was the *London Athletics Club*, founded in 1866. Following this a *National Olympian Association* covering the whole country held its first meeting in 1867 at Crystal Palace, London. It was at this match that the famous cricketer WG Grace slipped away from fielding in a cricket match at the Oval to run in the hurdles. He won - then went back to score a century at the Oval!

Olympic trials

Britain wasn't the only country interested in sport, especially since the discovery of Olympia had sparked a lot of interest in the ancient Olympic Games. People tried to revive them in America, England, France, Sweden, Germany and Greece before de Coubertin was successful.

By 1612, even before the 'discovery' of Olympia, an 'Olympik Games' had been staged in the Cotswold Hills and in 1620 there was a proposal for an 'amphitheatre' for 'Olympiads' (another way of saying Olympic Games) to be built in London.

Jeux Olympiques were held under the *Directoire* (the government of revolutionary France 1795-99) while French aristocrats were being guillotined in Paris.

In 1813 Barthold Georg Niebuhr made plans for an immense hall to be built in Rome where all future Olympic Games would be held. This plan was later changed to a hall for beggars to sleep in, although in the drawings the beggars seem to be wearing ancient Greek costume.

In 1859,1870,1875 and 1889 'Olympic' games were held in Greece. As well as athletic events they included the Ancient Greek game of trying to stand on a greasy goatskin filled with wine. But it was hard to get things properly organised in Greece at that time: at the 1859 games, held in a square in Athens, spectators were trampled by mounted police and one of the runners dropped dead during a race. But despite this and other set-backs, the founder of these games, a wealthy merchant called Evanghelios Zappas, left his fortune to fund further games.

Brookes's baby

De Coubertin especially liked the *Wenlock Olympics*. These were another version of the Games, held at Much Wenlock in Shropshire. They'd been going for forty years when de Coubertin saw them in 1889. He was invited by Dr Brookes, the founder of the games, who was an old man by then. The Wenlock Games started with a procession from a local pub, led by a herald wearing a red velvet cap with white feathers and carrying a banner in Greek. There were competitions for painting and writing as well as sporting events, and there were quotations in Greek and laurel wreaths for prizes. It was all based on the ancient Olympics with a bit of medieval stuff mixed in. Almost the only thing old Dr Brookes didn't like about the Ancient Greeks was their attitude towards women: in his games the ladies got the best seats and the champion jouster received his prize from a lady. (However women still didn't compete.) For his part, de Coubertin loved the prizes, the procession and the ceremonies. He made sure there was plenty of all of them when he started his own Games.

IT'S STARTED!

In 1884, five years after de Coubertin's visit to Much Wenlock, the modern Olympic movement was born.

The birth took place at a grand conference in Paris, a conference called by de Coubertin to discuss the start of an *international* Olympics to be held every four years. Sport-lovers from twelve countries came to the conference and twenty-one other countries sent messages of support. (At eighty-five, Dr Brookes was too old to get there.)

De Coubertin knew how to throw a party. Delegates were greeted with poems, speeches and champagne. They listened to a *Hymn to Apollo*, based on Ancient Greek music and arranged by the great composer Gabriel Fauré - two thousand people went to the concert. The sport lovers were invited to one party after another over several days. They watched fencing matches and running races while they sipped wine and listened to military music, they saw rowing races and a tennis championship. It all ended with a grand ceremony with fireworks.

And it was all a huge success. The sport-lovers decided to form an International Olympic Committee (IOC) with de Coubertin as its secretary , and it was agreed that the first modern Olympic Games would take place in Athens two years later.

ARE YOU AN OLYMPICS EXPERT?

Now that you've read this far, you've got a *sporting* chance of doing this quiz.
(Answers on page 122.)

1 What was de Coubertin's favourite book?

a The Bible

b Tom Brown's Schooldays

c The Axe-Masters of Planet Zog

2 What did de Coubertin see in Rugby Chapel?

a Thomas Arnold

b A squash match

c A vision

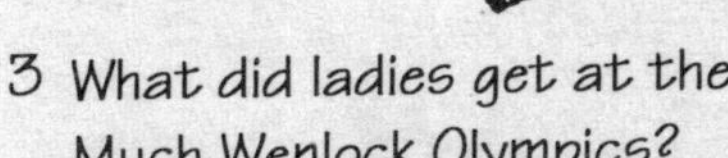

3 What did ladies get at the Much Wenlock Olympics?

a Lovely t-shirts printed with the letters 'MW'

b She-shirts

c The best seats

He became President in 1896.

ON YOUR MARKS!

TIME FOR THE REAL THING

WHAT A BUILD-UP!

Greece got busy. It was decided that the very first modern Olympics would be held in the ancient stadium of the Panathenaean Games in Athens (see page 11), which had forty-six rows of marble seats and could hold a crowd of 50,000. Naturally, after more than a thousand years it needed a little building work doing on it: a rich Greek called Georges Averoff stumped up £36,500 to pay for the renovation work.

By the time of the grand opening ceremony Greece had worked itself into a frenzy of excitement. All the public buildings of Athens were festooned with bunting, there were the initials 'oa' (the initials of 'Olympic Games' in Greek writing) everywhere. A crowd of 40,000 packed into the stadium, and another 60,000 filled the surrounding streets and spread over the nearby hills (in total, almost the entire population of Athens at that time). After the king [footnote] had proclaimed the Games open, a huge orchestra played the newly-composed *Olympic Hymn*.

[footnote] At that time Greece had a royal family. It's now a republic.

WHAT A BUNCH

The athletes were a mixed bunch. The British squad for instance included two of the embassy staff and a tourist who signed up for the tennis tournament at the last moment - and won. Among the Americans, Robert Garrett of Princetown University entered for the discus, but only reluctantly because he'd never thrown one before - and he won that. Among the French, an athlete called Albin Lermusiaux wore white gloves because he was running in front of the king!

IDIOT!

Amateurs, 'gentlemen' and professionals

Idiotes was the Ancient Greek word for a non-professional or ignorant person. It's where we get our word 'idiot' from.

The athletes at the first modern Olympics were *idiotes*: that is, they were non-professional and didn't compete for money but just for the love of sport. In sport, that's what 'amateur' means nowadays. De Coubertin believed that all ancient Greek athletes were amateurs, but he was wrong: they often made their living from sport and had no wish to be *idiotes* if there was money to be made. Since 1992 modern Olympic athletes have not had to be amateurs either.

In actual fact 'amateurism' has always been as much to do with *what class you are* as to *whether or not you want to make money from your sport*. After all, only the rich can afford not to work so as to have plenty of time for training. Way back in the 1850s, the runner John Astley claimed that, although he ran for money, he still thought of himself as an amateur, because he didn't need it. To him 'amateur' meant a gentleman and 'professional' meant a labourer or a 'tradesman'. In the rules of the Amateur Athletic Club , founded London 1866, the word 'amateur' was specially used so as to keep out working class athletes.

American John Kelly, who won the singles skulls in the rowing competition at Antwerp in 1920, wasn't allowed to row in the Henley Regatta because he was a bricklayer and so had an unfair advantage! He later became a millionaire and his daughter Grace Kelly became a famous film actress and, later, Queen of Monaco.

In 1872 the Amateur Athletic Club accepted a tradesman as a member and sixty members resigned in protest!

Carlo Airoldi of Italy travelled 1,500 kilometres on foot to the 1896 Athens Olympics, only to be barred from competing on charges of professionalism.

Jim Thorpe, a part-native-American athlete, was perhaps the greatest Olympic athlete of all time (see page 111). In 1912 he was barred for life from athletics and had all his medals taken away. This was because he had once received a small payment for a baseball game.

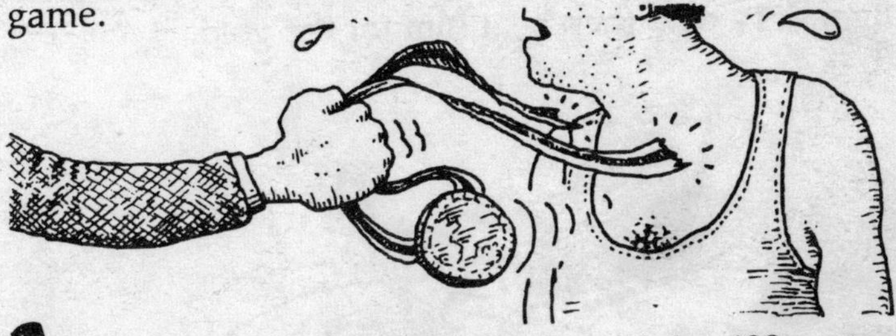

Irishman Robert Tisdall, winner of the 400 metres hurdles at the 1932 Los Angeles Olympics, was a true amateur, giving up his job and moving into a converted railway carriage where he lived with his wife on a pound a week, so as to be able to train. Not many people have that kind of dedication.

Gentleman amateurs liked to look as if they didn't care too much about their sport. Bevil Rudd, winner of the 400 metres in an early Oxford versus Cambridge meeting, laid down his cigar before the race, remarking when he picked it up afterwards that it was still 'burning nicely'.

Amateurs are meant to have a spirit of 'fair play' - like Eugenio Monti, the bobsled champion who gave his spare runners to the British pair in the 1964 Winter Olympics - who then beat him for the gold.

Go!

The very first event of the modern Olympic Games was the 100 metres, won by Thomas Burke, an American, who was thus the first ever gold medal winner.

After that the crowd was able to watch most of the same track and field events that are held today. It was all very friendly. It was also a bit disorganised and there were a few problems: the swimmers competed in the open sea of the Bay of Salamis where the waves were four metres high and the water was freezing.

Alfréd Hajós of Hungary, the winner of the 100 and 1,500 metres freestyle races, smeared his body with a layer of grease several centimetres thick to keep out the cold. He swam fast because he was terrified that he would drown! The yachting regatta was cancelled.

MARATHON

There was no marathon race in the ancient Olympics. The modern race is based on the famous run of an ancient Athenian who brought news of victory against the invading Persians at the Battle of Marathon in 490 BC. He is said to have run all the way to Athens, said: 'Rejoice, we conquer!', then died on the spot.

 In 1896 the actual distance they swam in the 1,500 metres was only 1,200 metres.

Excitement was high before the start in 1896: Marathon is a village 38.6 kilometres north-east of Athens and the entire route from the village was lined with spectators. Caught up in the excitement was a beautiful, wealthy Athenian girl, known to history as *Miss Y*, who promised to marry the victor whoever he was, as long as he was Greek.

Guess who won - a Greek! His name was Spyridon Louis and he was a tough, wiry shepherd - not at all the handsome hero that Miss Y had been expecting. She broke down in tears. Fortunately, Louis didn't accept her offer.

The Marathon was the high point of the Games. When Louis staggered exhausted into the stadium the whole crowd went mad with joy. The two royal princes, Constantine and George, rushed down and ran with him to the finishing line.

Prizes

Spyridon Louis was the hero of the hour. Over the following days he was offered all sorts of presents, but he turned them all down except for a horse and cart for carrying water in his village - and his olive branch, of course.

Until 1932 all awards were presented at the end of the Games in a special ceremony. Along with the other victors, Louis received his medal from the hand of the King. The King also presented the olive branches which were cut from trees at ancient Olympia. When the ceremony was over, the crowd rushed forward and grabbed every remaining leaf and twig to take home as souvenirs.

The first Olympics had been a big success. There was just one problem: the Greeks wanted the modern Olympics to be an *international* festival, but they wanted it always to be held in Greece and controlled by the Greeks - after all they'd been holding their own Games off and on since 1859. That was why the Greek King had put himself at the head of the festival, handing out awards and making speeches. In his final speech the King thanked his own son for helping set up the games - but he didn't thank de Coubertin.

ARE YOU AN OLYMPICS EXPERT?

Now that you've read this far, you've got a *sporting* chance of doing this quiz.

(Answers on page 122.)

1 Who was in the British squad in the first modern Olympics?

a An American called Robert Garrett
b A tourist
c The British ambassador

2 What were idiotes?

a Stupid Greeks
b Greek athletes
c Non-professionals

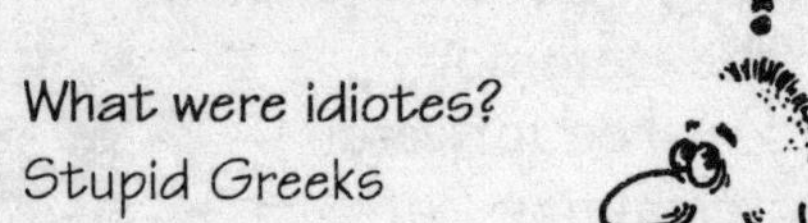

3 Why did Alfréd Hajós smear himself with grease?

a To keep out the cold
b To slide smoothly through the water
c It was a Greek marriage custom and he thought he looked good

4 What did Miss Y do?

a Promise to marry Spyridon Louis
b Promise to marry any Greek winner of the Marathon
c Fall madly in love with Spyridon Louis and live happily ever after

My, HOW YOU'VE GROWN!

FROM A BABY TO A BIG, FAT ADULT

HOME ALONE

Back in Paris, de Coubertin was determined that the Games would not always be held in Greece. And he had become President of the International Olympic Committee so he won the argument. The Greeks were only allowed what are known as the *Intercalated Games* which were meant to be held every four years between Olympics. As it turned out there was only ever one Intercalated Games, held in 1906.

Not that the dream of a permanent home for the Olympics in Greece is totally dead. Right now, some members of the Olympic Committee dream of carving a new mini-state out of the land of Greece, a permanent home where the Games can put down roots. Many Greeks are keen on the idea as well.

During the Second World War, Adolf Hitler dreamt of a permanent home for the Olympics in Berlin. He planned a huge stadium, big enough for 45,000 spectators.

MEASLY MEETINGS

In the early years it was far from sure that the Olympics would turn out to be the world's top sports meeting. Other sports meetings cropped up all over the place like measle-spots on a measle-sufferer. De Coubertin had to make sure that his Games were the most important.

In 1891 John Astley Cooper planned a *Pan-Britannic* and *Anglo-Saxon* Festival for athletes from the USA and the British Empire. This was meant to rival the Olympics and to show how superior Anglo-Saxons were. The plan never came off.

The first *Workers' Olympics* was held in Frankfurt, Germany, in 1925. Organised by socialists, 100,000 workers, both athletes and spectators, took part and it was a huge success. Three more Workers' Olympics were held over the following years.

In the early modern Olympics women were only allowed to compete in a few events, such as golf and tennis, so they set up their own international meeting. It was held in Paris in 1920 before a crowd of more than 20,000 spectators. Another Women's Olympics was planned for 1926, but then women were promised a real part in the next Olympic games due 1928.

Most modern athletic sports have their own international federations to decide on rules and other matters (see page 47). All these federations together form the *International Amateur Athletics Federation* (IAAF). Recently the IAAF has decided to hold World Cup athletics games every two years. The World Cup is the biggest threat to the Olympics as the world's number one sporting occasion so far.

Socialists believe, among other things, that workers should get their 'fair share' of power and wealth.

As it turned out, women were only allowed to compete in five track and field events. The British women were so disgusted with this that they stayed away.

DREAM BEAN

Right now the Olympics are still the biggest and the best. They've grown a lot since Athens 1896. In fact they're still growing like beans on fertilizer - runner beans. The same is true of the Winter Olympics, which were first held in 1924 at Chamonix, France.

It's difficult to keep down the number of athletes competing. First of all, there are always more and more sports waiting to be included; secondly, more and more countries are rich enough to send athletes; and thirdly, there's the basic fact that there are at least three times more people in the world now than there were in 1896. One answer is to limit the number of athletes each country can enter for each event. In 1908 the limit was twelve athletes per country per event, this has now gone down to three, and may go down to two.

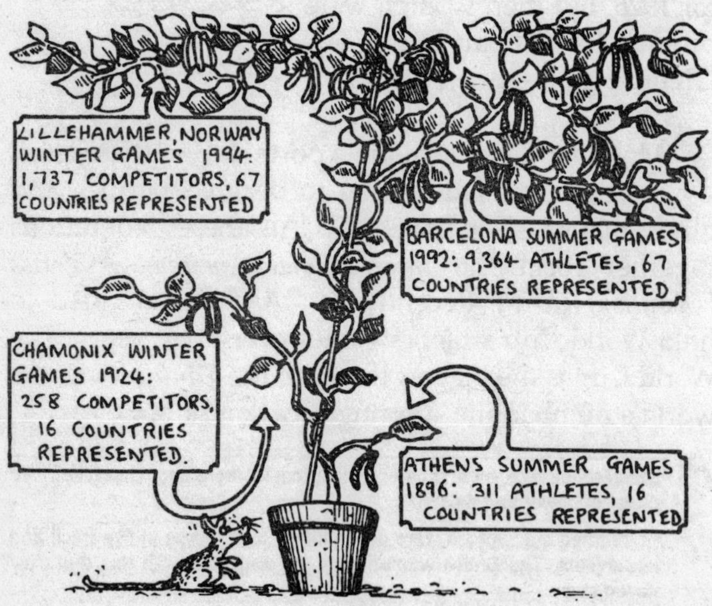

Bean scheme

A huge event like the Olympics takes a lot of organising. This is how it works:

Each country has its own *National Olympics Committee* (NOC), which decides which athletes should go to the Olympics and which city in their country can bid 👣 to host the Games. Together the National Committees form the *Association of National Olympic Committees* (ANOC).

Each sport has its own federation. They decide on the rules for all Olympic events. Together these federations form the *International Amateur Athletic Federation* (IAAF).

Running the whole show is the *International Olympics Committee*, started by the great man himself, Baron Pierre de Coubertin.

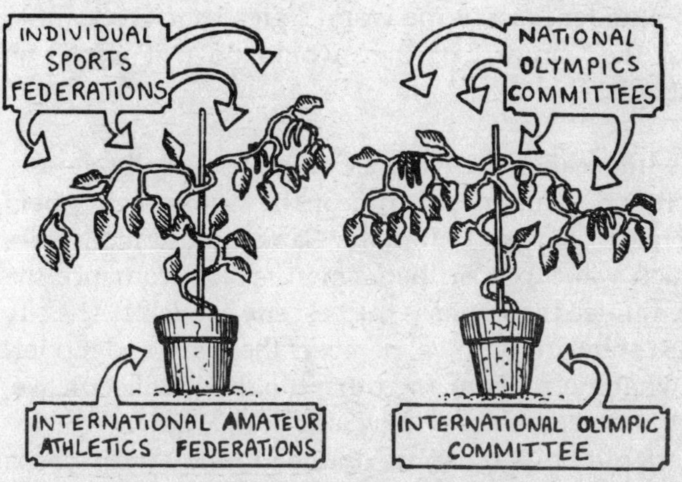

👣 *Bidding* is when different cities try to persuade the International Olympic Committee that their city should hold the games (see following page).

KEEP A LID ON THE BID

Imagine, your city will be the next host of the Olympic Games. Hundreds of thousands of athletes and spectators will flood in, they'll fill all the hotels and guest houses, they'll spend millions in the restaurants and shops. The whole world will be watching you - it'll be a bonanza!

No wonder most of the world's greatest cities want to host the Games - or they would do if it wasn't so difficult.

The International Olympic Committee usually chooses a city six years in advance of the Games being held there. So six years before the Games in question, cities which want to host the Games have to convince the Committee that theirs is the best city available. The city must show Committee members the plans and models of what the stadium and other buildings will look like, Committee members may ask to be flown over to check out how things are on the ground - it can cost a city more than *sixteen million pounds* just to make their 'bid', and in the end they may not win.

For the city which wins, the actual cost of getting ready is truly enormous: Barcelona spent more than *three billion* pounds before the 1992 Games. And they can still lose money by the end of it - the Montreal Olympics lost more than a billion dollars by the time the 1976 Games were over.

PUTTING A ROOF ON IT

Each host city tries to outdo the Games that went before. The buildings must be more daring, the opening ceremony more lavish.

- The roof of the stadium at the 1994 Lillehammer Winter Games was designed to look like an upside-down Viking ship. It was supported by the longest expanse of wooden beams in the world.

- The 1976 Montreal stadium had a retractable roof. (Except it wasn't finished until years after the Games were over!)

- At Munich in 1972, spectators walked under a 610-metre rainbow made of helium tubes, like a giant balloon.

TELLY SALES

Television is where most of the money for all the buildings and for the competition comes from. TV audiences are vast beyond imagining: *2,500 million people* switched on for parts of the 1984 Los Angeles Games.

It works like this: the organisers of the Games sell the right to screen the Games to a TV company, then that company sells advertising time to other companies to advertise their products. Companies will pay a lot to show their products to such a huge audience. At Los Angeles they paid up to 8,300 dollars for *each second* an advert was on TV.

It's all a long way from the first television broadcast at the 1936 Berlin Games, even though that was the world's first 'major' television broadcast. About 15,000 people watched the Berlin Games on twenty-seven flickering screens set up around the city.

SNACK BACKING

As well as television, the Games make money from sponsors. Sponsor companies pay to have their product made 'official'. For instance, Mars Bars were the 'official' snack food at the 1984 Los Angeles Games.

Most sports meetings have sponsors nowadays. The 1990 football World Cup in Rome should have been called the 'Adidas Cup': all games were played on Adidas balls, the referee and the linesmen were all kitted out by Adidas, so were both teams in the final and fifteen out of twenty-four teams in the rest of the competition - and Adidas provided the 'official' boot!

Anything that can be is sold to raise money for the Olympics. The organisers of the 1984 Los Angeles Games even sold the carrying of the Olympic torch (more on that later) at 3,000 dollars per kilometre of carrying! although, to be fair, the money went to charity.

It's ideal

Nowadays the Olympic games drink money like a big, expensive car drinks petrol. But although money is important, the dream of fair competition between countries and athletes has never died. As far as the Olympic Committee is concerned, an athlete is an athlete no matter what class or colour he or she is.

In fact it's against the rules for a country to choose its athletes by the colour of their skin. In 1959, South Africa said they would be sending an all-white team to the 1960 Rome Games. They claimed that they weren't practising racial discrimination - that it just so happened that all their best athletes were white! The International Olympic Committee didn't agree. South Africa lost the argument and they didn't get to the Olympics.

SPORTY CENTURY

RUNDOWN OF THE GAMES FROM 1896-1996

GAMES GAME - FOR STUPID PEOPLE

There have been twenty-three modern Olympic Games. There are twenty-six Games shown below: which three were cancelled because of war?

Answer Berlin 1916, Tokyo 1940, London 1944

Sports snippets

Check out these cuttings from the *Record Times*.

1900 Paris

SHORT CUT SUSPECTED

American runners in the marathon, having taken an early lead, have been puzzled as to how the French overtook them to win the race. The French runners were not covered in mud like everyone else. Rumour says that the French took a short cut through the narrow back streets of Paris.

1900 Paris

WHAT A MIX-UP!

The Olympics are to be held as part of a big trade exhibition and have been renamed by the exhibition organisers, so they are no longer the 'Olympic Games' or the *Jeux Olympiques* as they are known in France 👣. Ice skaters are listed as part of the cutlery exhibition! Small wonder some athletes have returned home without realising that they have competed in the Olympics!

1900 Paris

ONLY SEVEN

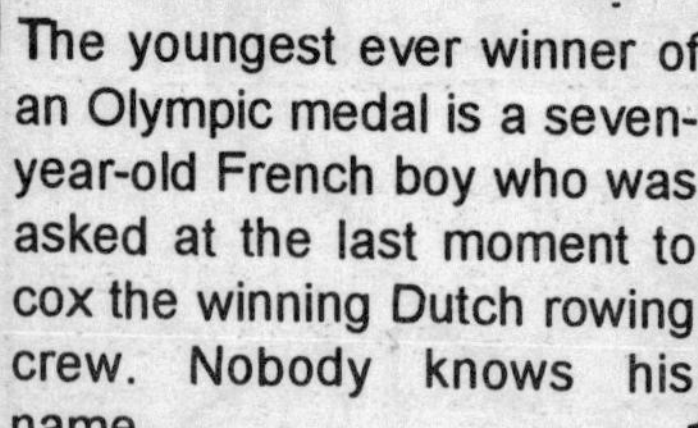

The youngest ever winner of an Olympic medal is a seven-year-old French boy who was asked at the last moment to cox the winning Dutch rowing crew. Nobody knows his name.

1900 Paris

PIT STOP

Athletics events are being held in the Bois de Boulogne. All jumpers are advised to bring a spade since they may have to dig their own pits.

👣 The trade exhibition was called the *Exposition Universelle* and the Olympic games were renamed the *Concours Internationaux d'Exercises Physiques et de Sport (International PT and Sport Competition).*

1900 Paris

S-COOPED IT!

Charlotte Cooper of Great Britain, the winner of the women's tennis title, is the first ever female gold medallist.

1900 Paris

SLIPPED DISC

Robert Garrett, USA, winner of the 1896 gold medal, has hurled all three of his discus throws into the crowd! No one is reported to have been injured by his poor aim.

1900 Paris

FISH DISH

Angling for live fish in the River Seine has been suggested for part of the Olympic programme.

1900 Paris

GO WITH THE FLOW

Swimming with the current in the River Seine, Australian Frederick Lane has been swept along so fast that he has chopped thirteen seconds off the 200 metres world freestyle record!

1904 St. Louis

A SNIP OFF THE OLD BLOCK

When Cuban postman Felix Carvajal turned up for the start of the marathon in heavy walking shoes and long trousers, something had to be done to help him run the race. That's why a friendly American trimmed his trouser legs with a pair of scissors. Felix is said to have lost all his money in a game of dice in New Orleans. He then begged his way to St Louis and arrived without proper equipment. He didn't win!

1904 St Louis

TRACK LACK

Lack of interest from many countries has led to high numbers of local American athletes winning prizes. Out of 554 competitors, 432 were American. The British and French have sent no athletes at all, and in some events only Americans have competed. These games, held as part of a trade fair to celebrate a hundred years since the *Louisiana Purchase* , have dragged on for months and months.

1908 London

NOT ON SUNDAY

The final of the 110 metres hurdles has been delayed due to the refusal of favourite, Forrest Smithson, to run on a Sunday. He is said to have run eventually - but carrying a Bible! He won gold.

1920 Antwerp

OUR FLAG

The Olympic flag, designed by Baron Pierre de Coubertin based on an Ancient Greek artefact, has been flown for the first time. The interlacing rings stand for the five continents of the world and for friendship between countries.

1908 London

MARATHON LENGTH FIXED

For the benefit of the watching Royal children, the marathon is to start beneath the windows of Windsor Castle .

In 1803 the USA bought the territory of *Louisiana* from France for $27,267,622.

From 1924 the 42,195 metres from Windsor Castle to the stadium became the standard length of the marathon, instead of the distance of 35,000 metres from the village of Marathon to Athens.

1920 Antwerp

UGH!

Paavo Nurmi, the 'Flying Finn' 👣 has won his first ever gold medal in the 10,000 metres race. Very unfortunately, poor Joseph Guillemot the silver medallist was sick all over Nurmi just after he crossed the finishing line two seconds later.

1932 Los Angeles

COWBOY COUNTRY

The very first Olympic village, providing 550 houses for male athletes, is to be guarded by cowboys who will patrol the outer fence. The French will be allowed wine to drink with their meals, although alcohol has been illegal in the USA since 1919. The women athletes will be housed separately at a hotel in town.

1936 Barcelona

POPULAR OLYMPICS

Disgusted that the games are to be held in Adolf Hitler's Berlin, the citizens of Barcelona have held their own *Popular Olympics* with 5,000 athletes and 20,000 spectators. Sadly, the games have come to a sudden end only a day after they started, because a violent military uprising has signalled the start of the Spanish Civil War.

1936 Berlin

TORCH FIRST

For the first time, 3,000 runners in relays will carry a living flame from the site of ancient Olympia to the Berlin Stadium. In addition, at the opening ceremony a vast 16.76 tonne bell will be rung and the music will be conducted by the famous composer Richard Strauss.

👣 More on him later.

1936 Berlin

VILE HITLER!

Nazi Chancellor Adolf Hitler is said to be furious at the success of ten black American athletes. The black athletes have won seven gold, three silver and three bronze medals. Hitler was hoping that the Berlin Games would show that white, German athletes are the best. He is said to be especially angry that the German crowd cheered Jesse Owens.

1936 Berlin

DOCUMENTARY

Leni Riefenstahl has produced a stunning documentary about the Olympic Games. Although her film was paid for by the Nazi propaganda office, Riefenstahl has focused on the black American champion, Jesse Owens from Alabama, who has won four gold medals in four days.

1948 Hollywood

THE LAST TARZAN

Johnny Weissmuller, star of nineteen Tarzan films from 1932, has announced that he is to retire from film making this year. Before he became a film star, Johnny was a champion swimmer, winning gold in the 100 and 400 metres freestyle and the 4×200 metres relay in the 1924 Paris Olympics, and in the 100 metres freestyle in the 1928 Amsterdam Games.

At the same Games, child specialist Dr Benjamin Spock won gold in the rowing eights.

1956 Melbourne

BLOODY WATER!

Following the recent, ruthless Russian invasion of Hungary, the Hungarian water polo team had a score to settle in their semi-final against the Russians. The game became so rough that blood coloured the water and the Russians abandoned play.

1968 Mexico

BLACK POWER

Black American medallists of the 200 metres have raised black-gloved hands in a 'black power' salute at the awards ceremony. As sprinter John Carlos said: 'If I win I'm an American, not a black American; if I did something bad they would call me a negro.' Later the black 400 metre squad did the same thing, this time wearing black berets.

1972 Munich

MURDER

Nine Israeli athletes have been shot dead by Palestinian terrorists at Munich airport. The terrorists entered the Israeli rooms in the Olympic village during the night. It has been decided that the Games will go on, to show that terrorism will not succeed.

ATHLETE'S FOOT

TIME TO GET STARTED (AGAIN!)

Go!

Foot racing at the ancient Olympics began as a sacrifice to the gods. In those far-off days the priests of Elis used to stack sticks round sacrificial gifts of meat and fruit. A signal was then given to a crowd of boys waiting about 200 metres away. The boys raced to be first to grab a flaming torch from the hand of a priest and to light the sticks, thus burning the meat and fruit as a sacrifice.

This religious ceremony grew into the earliest of all events at the ancient Olympics, the *stadium race* of 192 metres . Running races were always at the heart of the ancient Games - and they still are today. And the first thing you do when running a race is to start it:

The 100 metres was the first event of the modern Games (see page 38).

Ancient Greek runners seem to have started with one foot a few centimetres in front of the other.

At the 1896 Athens Olympics some runners used starting sticks.

Starting blocks were introduced in 1929.

The crouch start is said to have been invented by Bobby Macdonald in 1884, a runner of New Zealand Maori origin.

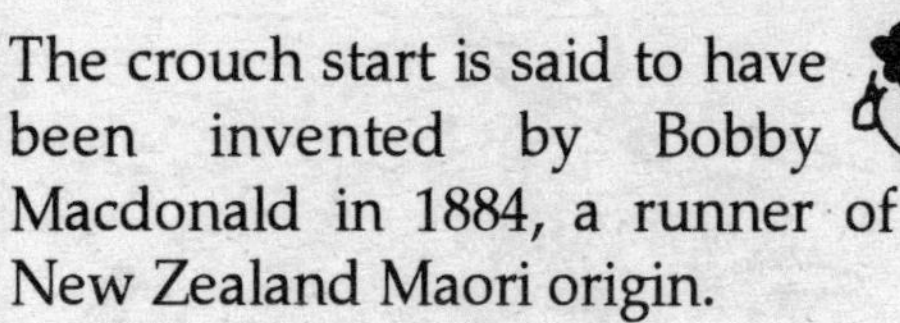

Many runners used a starting hole.

Until 1912 the sprint lanes were divided by ropes not by chalk lines on the ground.

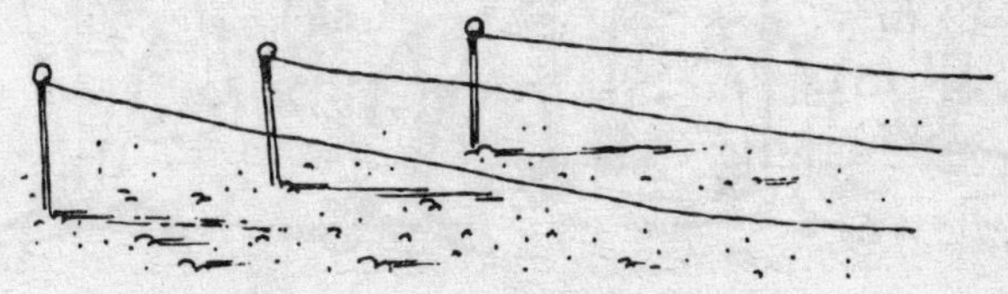

PLACE THE RACE

Most of these runners know which race they're running in because they've got it written on them in case they forget. The different races of the modern

Olympic programme are all written in squares on the track. But one runner hasn't got a race because his or her distance isn't in the programme: which distance is it?

Answer on page 122

Hurdles races started in England. The early hurdles were solidly-made sheep barriers. The official height of the 110m men's hurdles is still 0.914 metres.

There was no relay race in the ancient Olympics, although the Ancient Greeks did run torch races. Naked men would carry the torches from one altar to another. Spectators would laugh as the runners tried to keep the torches alight and would speed them on their way with friendly (or not-so-friendly) slaps.

It's a record!

The Ancient Greeks didn't care how long it took to run a race so long as they won it. The idea of keeping a *record* of the *speed* of a race started in England in the seventeenth century. It was all to do with betting: the English were just as happy to bet on the time a runner took to run a race as on who won it. The first athletics record book was probably the 'betting book' at a famous gambling club in London called White's.

The English would bet on anything, but running races were a specially popular sport among seventeenth- and eighteenth-century English gamblers. The runners, known as *pedestrians* , used to run on the same tracks as the racehorses. The best of them tended to be *footmen*. A footman's usual job was to carry messages between the town and country houses of the rich. On the dreadful roads of that time, a good footman could travel far faster than the family coach

The Latin for a foot-soldier is *pedes*. A *pedestrian* is someone who goes on foot and not on horseback or in a car.

and sometimes even faster than a man on horseback. Fast footmen were bought and sold like footballers today so that their masters could race them against other footmen.

By the seventeenth century there were more bets about making or beating records than about winning or losing races. One of the most famous bets of all time was by Captain Barclay Allardice. In 1808 he bet £1000 that he could walk 1000 miles in 1000 hours. He walked round the racecourse at Newmarket and finished well in time. He won £16,000, which at its modern value is probably as much money as has ever been earned by a sportsman for a single event.

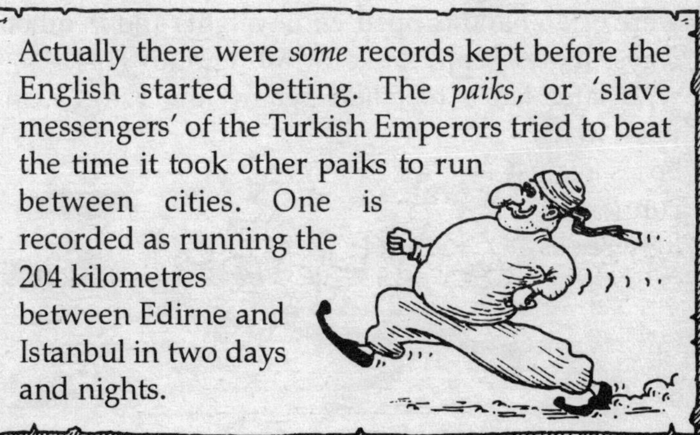

Actually there were *some* records kept before the English started betting. The *paiks*, or 'slave messengers' of the Turkish Emperors tried to beat the time it took other paiks to run between cities. One is recorded as running the 204 kilometres between Edirne and Istanbul in two days and nights.

Get the bet

The English were bonkers about betting. Here are some of the things they bet on:

A race between men with wooden legs, watched by King Charles II (1630-85).

Walking backwards for a mile.

In 1749 a man ran naked in St James' Park, London for a bet. Ladies threw coins and pretended to hide behind their fans.

In order to make things fairer from the point of view of betting, both horses and human runners were often handicapped with weights and in other ways. James Scott, Duke of Monmouth (1649-85), who later led a rebellion against the King, won races in his boots against runners in light shoes.

Marking time

Records are much better kept nowadays than they were in the days of the pedestrians, especially since the first *chronograph* or stop-watch was invented in 1862. Since the time of the Stockholm Olympics of 1912, electric time-keeping equipment has allowed athletes to measure records by tiny fractions of a second. This equipment has made possible many famous records, such as that of Doctor Roger Bannister, who beat the 'four-minute mile' at Oxford in 1954 - he finished his mile in 0.6 of a second less than four minutes! That's about the blink of an eyelid.

FURTHER FIELD EVENTS

WHAT TO DO IN THE STADIUM IF YOU'RE NOT RUNNING

Running is just one of the things athletes do in the Olympic arena. There's always plenty of hopping, jumping and throwing going on in the background while the races are being run. The throwing and jumping are the other *field* events, so called because they take place on the 'field'. Let's focus on these other events:

YOU'RE FOR THE HIGH JUMP!

There was no high jump in the ancient Olympics, no Fosbury Flop, no belly-roll, no western roll, no Horine Style. Even today it's a difficult event because the waiting time between jumps makes the athletes nervous - there are so many people watching. Few world records for high jump have been broken at the Olympic games.

Named after *Dick Fosbury* who won gold at the Mexico Games in 1968 by leaping backwards over the bar.

Called after American George Horine who had to practise running at the bar from the left because his back garden was so small.

They had sole

At the 1952 Helsinki Games the Russian jumpers wore shoes with extra high soles on whichever foot they jumped from. 'Orthopaedic' shoes have now been banned.

The long and the short of it

Long jump is an ancient sport. Cuchulain, an Ancient Irish champion, was famous for his 'salmon leap' in which he appeared to make a second leap while still in mid air. The Ancient Greeks used small weights called *halteres* to increase the length of their long jumps. By swinging a pair of weights it's possible to increase the length of a jump by more than a third.

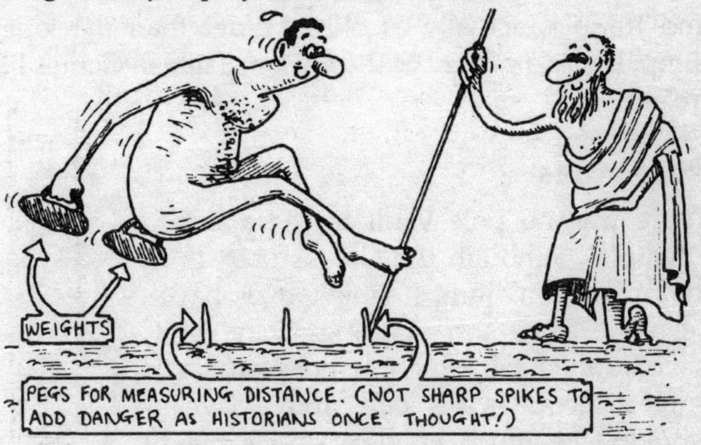

By the time of George Washington (1732-99), the first president of the USA, who was a good long jumper in his youth, weights had long since fallen out of use. Modern long jumpers must rely on the speed of their run more than anything else, which is why many of the best long jumpers are also champion sprinters, such as Jesse Owens who won gold at the 1936 Berlin Games and Carl Lewis who won it at the Seoul Games in 1988.

The world record for long jump is 8.95m (Mike Powell USA, Tokyo 1991) at the time of writing, but the world record for the *triple jump* is 18.93m (Jonathan Edwards GB, Gothenburg 1995) - which is hardly surprising since the triple jump is three jumps one after the other.

The triple jump which used to be called the Hop, Step and Jump is actually as old or older than the long jump. It was an event at the ancient Tailtean Games in Ireland.

Pole voles

There was no pole vault in the ancient Olympics, although the Greeks used to go in for 'javelin' jumps which may have been the same sort of thing. They can't have vaulted very high: a pole vaulter is only as good as his pole and a javelin wouldn't be much good against a bendy bamboo pole such as were in use by 1910. And bamboo is no match for fibre glass or carbon fibre, which are what the best modern poles are made from.

It's an old sport: poles were used for jumping water channels in the fen district of East Anglia for hundreds of years and pole vaulting was a popular English sport in the sixteenth century. But it wasn't until the mid 1800s that Ulverston Cricket Club in the Lake District decided to try pole vaulting as a modern athletic event. The Ulverston cricketers used heavy ash or hickory poles with three iron spikes at one end and competitors could climb the pole as well as swinging on it. This was the traditional method of vaulting, but climbing was eventually banned around 1900.

Shot to pieces

Famous hammer-throwers:

Hammer-throwing is as old as the Tailtean Games. The first hammers were real hammers, but the modern 'hammer' must be a metal ball of at least 7.26kg attached to a grip by steel wire. It's weighed the same ever since 1866 when the event was included in the very first Amateur Athletics Association meeting in England. This is a sport for the muscle men and it's always been dangerous - if the hammer flies off in the wrong direction!

SHOT SPOT

The shot is a metal ball of the same weight as the hammer but without the wire and the grip. Women also put the shot, their shot is 4kg. It's been popular for centuries, in fact during the reign of Edward III (1312-77) shot-putting was banned in England because it was feared that it was getting in the way of men practising their archery! The circular launch platform was first used in the 1904 St Louis Games when a huge American called Ralph Rose competed against fellow Americans (it being the St Louis Games there weren't many other countries competing). Rose is described as holding the shot in the palm of his huge hand 'like a marble'. He won gold.

TALL BALL FALL

'Shot' is another word for a missile fired from a gun or a cannon, such as a cannon-ball. In the early part of the twentieth century a German woman called Kätchen Brumbach (known as 'Catherine the Great') could throw cannon balls of 13.6kg up to nine metres in the air and then catch them on the back of her neck as they fell.

ANYONE FOR DISCBEE?

Discus was popular among the Ancient Greeks and was one of the main events in the ancient Olympics. Their discuses weighed from 1.75 to 4kg. The modern discus weighs at least 2kg and in most other ways is a copy of the ancient item.

Nowadays athletes make a complicated double turn on the small launch platform before releasing the discus. The real secret is to make sure it leaves the hand flat and spinning so that it sails through the air like an over-weight frisbee and gains extra distance.

JAVELIN

No doubt there have been javelin competitions for as long as people have been killing each other with spears - a javelin is a light throwing spear. But in the old days javelins were often thrown at targets. It was in the late nineteenth century that the Hungarians and Germans started throwing for distance only. It's their sport which has grown into the modern event.

The javelin was an important event in the ancient Olympics, and the athletes probably threw much longer distances than modern ones do. This is because they used a throwing thong or *amentum*, a short strip of leather which was wound round the centre of the javelin.

When released from an amentum a javelin spins in flight. Experiments under the French Emperor Napoleon (1769-1821) showed that an athlete who could only throw 25 metres unaided could throw 65 metres when he used an amentum - so it makes quite a difference!

In 1956 the Spaniards tried to reintroduce the amentum, but it was banned because people thought it was too dangerous.

In fact, the javelin being a weapon of war, it can always be dangerous if it flies too far or in the wrong direction. In 1986 a new advanced aluminium model was also banned because it could be thrown right out of a standard athletics field!

PENTATHWOT?

In the ancient Olympics the *pentathlon* combined running, jumping, javelin, discus and wrestling, but it was never very popular. The last modern Olympic pentathlon of this type took place in 1924. Since then that pentathlon has been replaced by the *heptathlon*, or 'contest of seven events'. The *decathlon* is a contest of ten events. On the first day the decathletes do the 100m sprint, long jump, shot-put, high jump and 400m, on the second day they do 110m hurdles, discus, pole vault, javelin and 1,500m. At the end of all that even the fittest athletes are totally exhausted!

Decathletes seem to be drawn to filming:

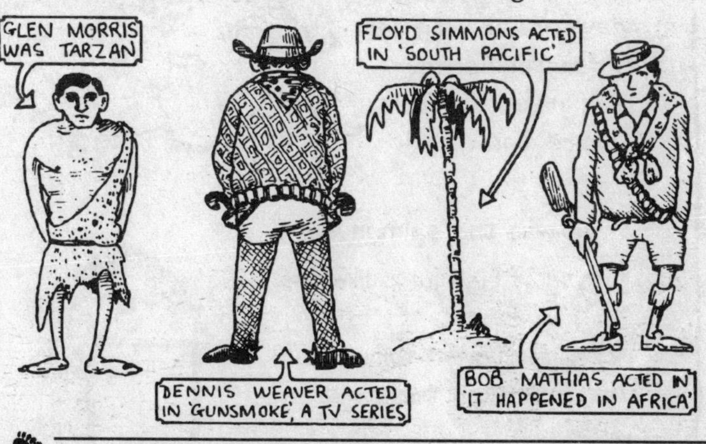

Pentathlon comes from the Ancient Greek *pente*, meaning 'five' and *athlon*, meaning 'contest'. The modern pentathlon combines riding, fencing, swimming, shooting and cross-country running.

ARE YOU AN OLYMPICS EXPERT?

Now that you've read this far, you've got a *sporting* chance of doing this quiz. (Answers on page 122.)

1 What did footmen do?

a Kick people
b Carry messages
c Walk slowly

2 Why did a man run naked in Saint James' Park in 1749?

a For a bet
b Because he was hot
c So as to run more quickly

3 What did Emperor Achmat do?

a Run 204km in two days and two nights
b Throw the hammer
c Run naked in Saint James' Park

4 What was the 'salmon leap'?

a A type of high jump like the 'Fosbury Flop'
b A sporting event for salmon
c The long jump technique of Cuchulain

HE MEN AND HIT MEN

WANNA FIGHT?

IT'S JUST SPORT

Fighting stops being 'fighting' and becomes sport once it has rules. Some fighting sports, fencing for instance, are fairly safe but others can be very bloody. Most countries have had some bloody sports. In one early Chinese sport, popular around 600 BC, the contestants put ox-skins over their heads, horns and all, and then butted each other until, as an ancient account puts it: 'there were smashed heads, broken arms and blood running in the palace yard' - but it was still a 'sport'! The same goes for Roman gladiators; they considered their fighting a sport even though it usually ended in death.

There are no really bloody sports in the modern Olympics - not like the ancient Olympics ...

Free fist hits

Boxing was said to be the favourite sport of the Ancient Greeks and it was certainly a big event at the ancient Olympics. In the early years boxers fought with bare fists but later they wound strips of soft leather round their knuckles. There were no rounds, no divisions between heavyweight and lightweight fighters, there was no ring and no rule against hitting a man when he was down. The contestants fought until both were too exhausted to carry on or until one or the other held up his hand to show that he was beaten. If a fight went on too long they might agree to give each other 'free hits'. That meant standing with your arms by your sides and letting your opponent smash you one in the face - and hoping that you survived to smash him one back when it was your turn.

The problem was - there wasn't enough blood. So they invented 'sharp thongs' which ringed the knuckles with a strip of hard leather. Later, the Romans improved on this with the *caestus*. The caestus was basically sharp thongs - with spikes! Strangely, the thumb was uncovered and could not be used in case it caused ugly wounds - it's hard to imagine what a thumb could do which spikes couldn't!

There wasn't much skill needed when boxing with sharp thongs or a *caestus*. After all, one blow was often enough to finish the fight. Defence became all important. One boxer called Melancomas could hold his guard for two days continuously, until his opponents would give in without any blows at all having been struck.

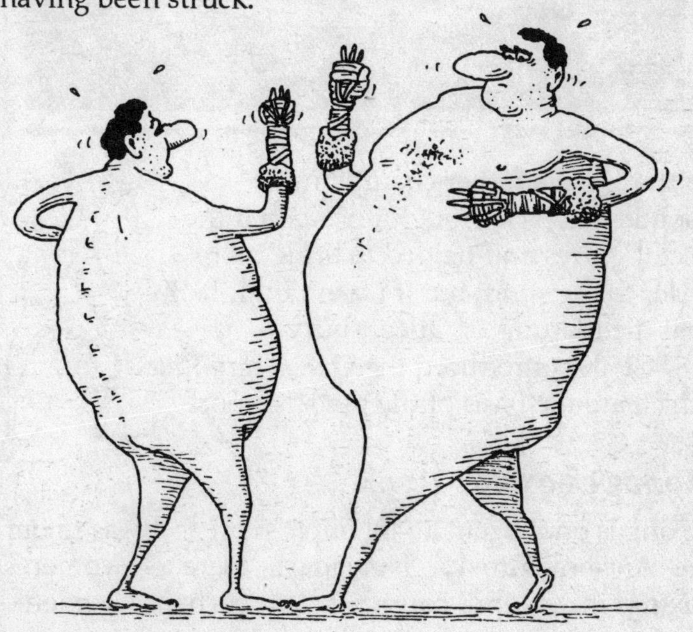

It's the rule!

The rules of modern boxing developed in Britain from the seventeenth century onwards. James Figg, 'the Great Figg' (died 1736), made the first rules although it was still a brutal sport in his day. He opened an 'amphitheatre' in London in 1719 and the first international was fought there between Englishman John Whitacker and Stopa l'Aqua, a boxer from Italy who 'never failed to smash his opponent's jaw bone'. (Whitacker won.)

In the 1740s another champion, 'Gentleman Jack Broughton', started the use of gloves and helped to bring more order to the sport, but it wasn't until 1867 that the Marquis of Queensbury (1844-1900) introduced the *Queensbury Rules* which are the basis of the modern sport.

Modern boxing

Boxing is once again an Olympic sport as it was under the Ancient Greeks. Nowadays there is women's boxing in several countries, so perhaps women's boxing will become an Olympic event before long.

Several world boxing champions have started out as amateurs who first won gold at the Olympics before going professional. The greatest of these is Cassius Clay, who later changed his name to Mohammed Ali. Ali won gold as a light heavyweight at the Rome Games in 1960. He's a black American. Back home in America, some time after the Games, he and a friend were attacked by two racists (it's hard to think of a worse person to attack, however tough those racists were!). Ali and his friend beat them, but he was so disgusted that he threw his medal into the Ohio River which happened to be nearby. 'My holiday as a white hope was over,' as he put it.

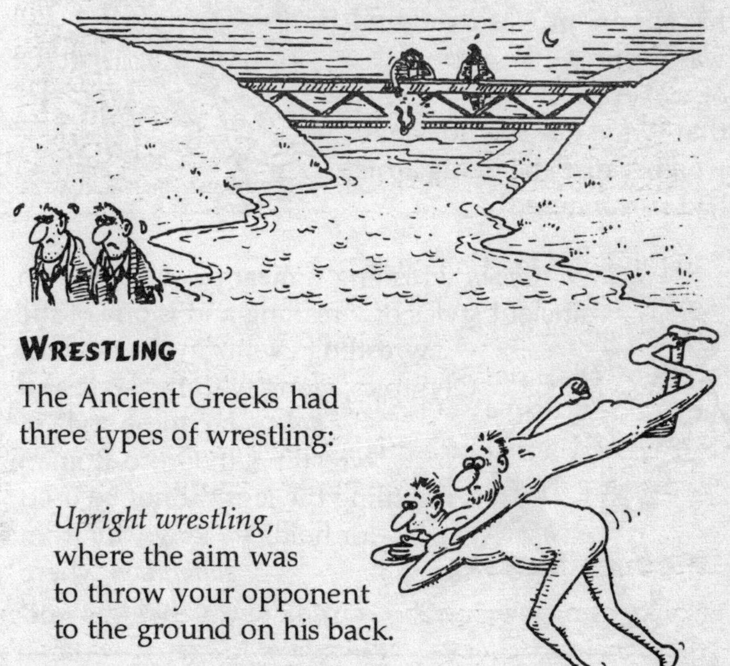

Wrestling

The Ancient Greeks had three types of wrestling:

Upright wrestling, where the aim was to throw your opponent to the ground on his back.

Ground wrestling, where the struggle went on until someone gave up. For ground wrestling the earth was watered so that it became muddy and slippery and it was difficult to keep a grip on your opponent.

Pankration, which was halfway between boxing and all-in wrestling. Sometimes even biting and gouging were allowed, and strangling was specially recommended. It was a brutal sport: in one Olympic contest a fighter tapped his opponent's shoulder - the signal for surrender - only to find that his opponent was dead and he was tapping the shoulder of a corpse. It was the corpse that was judged to have won because the living athlete had surrendered!

Greco-Roman wrestling is meant to be based on ancient styles of wrestling and is one of the wrestling events in the modern Olympics, along with freestyle and *judo*, a Japanese style of wrestling. In Greco-Roman wrestling the legs cannot be used for holds - a long way from *pankration* where *anything* could be used!

Japanese experts in *jujitsu* (another form of unarmed combat) develop the muscles of the throat so as to be able to resist strangleholds.

Because boxing and wrestling are dangerous sports the contestants are divided by weight so that men of roughly equal size fight each other. That way small, light men get a chance to compete as well as big, heavy men. Perhaps one of the greatest Olympic wrestlers was Ivar Johansson, a Swedish policeman. At Los Angeles in 1932 he won gold in the freestyle middle weight. It took him four bouts over three days. Then he stopped eating for twenty-four hours and sweated like a pig in a sauna so that he lost nearly 5kg and could wrestle in the Greco-Roman welterweight category - where he won gold again.

In the early modern Olympics there was no limit to the length of wrestling bouts. At the Stockholm Games in 1912 a contest was stopped after it had gone on for nine hours (both contestants were given silver).

WEIGHT-LIFTING

Weight-lifting was a popular sport among the Ancient Greeks, even though there was no weight-lifting competition at the ancient Olympics. Milo was a famous strongman who once carried a four-year-old cow round the stadium at Olympia. He then felled it with a single blow to the head and is said to have eaten the entire carcass in a day (actually that's impossible). He built his strength by carrying a calf on his shoulders, growing stronger as it grew.

Big eating is still necessary among modern weight-lifters. Tommy Kono, who won gold as a lightweight at Helsinki in 1952, used to eat up to seven meals a day if he needed to put on weight. If he wanted to lose weight he would cut down to just three meals a day. He won the Mr Universe competition in 1955 and 1957.

 He later married the daughter of the famous philosopher Pythagoras.

On guard!

Fencing is not as dangerous as it used to be. There was a time when young 'blades' would go to the theatre just so as to insult people, pick fights and kill them.

But it's still an incredibly fast and exciting sport, even though today there are 'buttons' to cover the end of the blades and all hits are counted electronically. However it can still be dangerous: in the 1980 Moscow Games Vladimir Lapitsky, the Russian champion, was pierced through the chest by the foil of his opponent, which only narrowly missed his heart.

And in 1924 after the Paris Olympics of that year, an Italian competitor and a Hungarian judge fought a duel for two hours until separated by their friends who were worried about the amount of blood they had spilled.

ARCHERY

Modern bows are made of a mixture of fibre glass and carbon fibre around a core of glass beads and foam. Wooden arrows flighted with eagle or turkey feathers have been replaced by carbon-wrapped aluminium rods. The modern equipment is very accurate - and deadly if not handled with care. Back in 1900 the old wooden arrows were deadly enough. Some claim that live pigeon shooting was an event at the 1900 Paris Games. Nowadays pigeons are left in peace; the archers only shoot at targets, at distances of from 30 to 90 metres.

There are other ways of using a bow for sport apart from shooting at a target. Turkish archers competed for distance, not accuracy. A Turkish champion called Toz Koparan Iskander could shoot 871 metres - that's more than half a mile.

It took a lot of strength to pull an old-fashioned wooden bow. The force needed to pull the toughest bow ever pulled was 78kg, done by Harold Hill who was part Cherokee native American.

BACK TO THE HAMMER ...

Shooting has always been part of the modern Olympics, but no event with guns more powerful than a small-bore rifle is allowed. That rules out anti-tank guns - and tossing the handgrenade, which the Belgians suggested for the Antwerp Olympics of 1920.

One of the most unpleasant Olympic shooters was James Snook who won gold in the free pistol team event at Antwerp in 1920. Nine years later he killed his mistress with a hammer and was executed in the electric chair.

A quick slip through the Winter Games

The Winter Olympics are smaller than the Summer Games, which is hardly surprising since most countries have very little snow and even less ice. It's unusual for a hot country like Jamaica to send many competitors to the Winter Olympics.

The first Winter Olympics were held at Chamonix in France in 1924, and in that same year the Summer Games were held in Paris. De Coubertin had had the idea that the same country should hold both Summer and Winter Games. This was crazy because it ruled out most countries in the world, which can never put on the Winter Games because of their climate. So from 1928 the Winter and Summer Games have always been held in different countries, but in the same year.

Only two Winter Games have ever been cancelled: the Games of 1940 and 1944, both because of World War II. There was just one other near miss. At Innsbruck, Austria, in 1964, there was so little snow that the Games were only saved when three thousand soldiers hauled 40,000 cubic metres of snow up to the ski and sleigh runs.

Skiing

Skiing is perhaps the oldest winter sport. There may have been a *Northern Games* in Scandinavia around 1800 BC, as early as the Tailtean Games. If there was a Northern Games at this date it's likely that skiing was included. Skadi, a very early northern goddess, was said to hunt on skis. She was the daughter of the ice giant, Thiassi.

Early skiing was all cross-country - skiers just plodded across the vast northern wastes. There was no ski-jumping until 1862 and the very first downhill race wasn't held until 1911. It takes a lot of courage to compete in the jumping and the downhill events: if you're not prepared to set off like a bat out of hell you may as well forget it. Speeds of up to nearly 65 mph (104.532 km/h) have been recorded on the downhill course, average times having more than doubled since 1936. Likewise the length of ski jumps has also doubled.

There are two types of hill in the jumping competitions: 90m and 120m. The longest jump ever recorded (at the time of writing) was from the 120m hill, a distance of 135.5 metres in 1994 at Lillehammer in Norway. That's a long way to jump!

LOVE TO SKATE

Figure skating is the glamour event of the Winter Olympics. After her victory in the 1984 women's figure skating Katarina Witt received *35,000* love letters.

Other figure skating champions, such as Sonja Henie (see page 114), have become film stars. But despite the glamour it takes a lot of courage and hard work to become a champion. Sonja practised eight hours a day from the age of seven. After she became rich and famous she answered a begging letter by saying that the secret of success was easy: you just had to work eighteen hours a day. (All right - she was exaggerating.)

Figure skating is one of the few events where what a competitor looks like may be important. Before the 1980 Lake Placid Games, the American Linda Fratianne had plastic surgery on her nose. She lost anyway, to the German Anett Pötzsch.

On the other hand, looks are totally unimportant for speed skating. Apart from anything else the competitors are almost completely sheathed in wind-resistant clothing, to reduce drag from the air rushing past them. This fashion started in 1962 when a Canadian skater beat the world record by three seconds wearing a pair of his wife's nylon stockings - you don't get love letters by dressing like that.

Sledge Section

The winning team at the 1932 two-man bobsled event heated the runners of their sled with a blowtorch before the race began. This practice is now illegal and in 1968 the East German women were disqualified for doing the same thing.

Ivan Brown, a gold medallist at the 1936 Games, was very superstitious: he believed it was lucky to find at least one hairpin every day. He found one on each of the twenty-four days before the final - so maybe his superstition was right.

The 1992 Jamaican bobsled team practised on push carts in the snowless Blue Mountains of Jamaica.

ARE YOU AN OLYMPICS EXPERT?

Now that you've read this far, you've got a *sporting* chance of doing this quiz.
(Answers on page 123.)

1 What were sharp thongs?

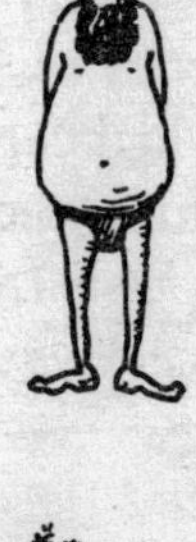

a Very brief uncomfortable underwear worn by ancient athletes

b A strip of hard leather wound round a boxer's knuckles

c Boxing gloves with spikes

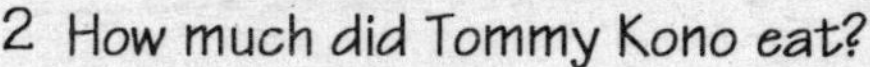

2 How much did Tommy Kono eat?

a Seven meals a day

b Twelve meals a day

c A light snack for breakfast, nothing for lunch and dinner of a carrot with low-fat yoghurt

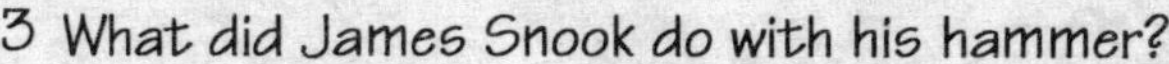

3 What did James Snook do with his hammer?

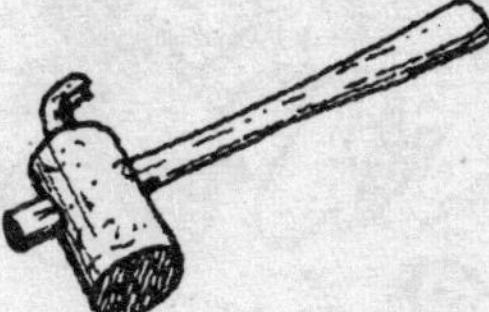

a Throw it

b Bang nails with it

c Kill his mistress with it

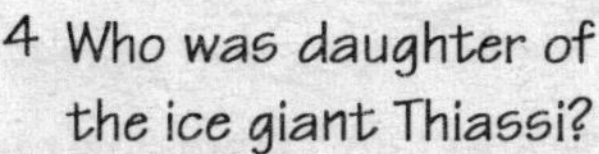

4 Who was daughter of the ice giant Thiassi?

a Katerina Witt

b Anett Pötzsch

c Skadi

It may happen event-ually

Olympic events take place on the ground, in water, on snow and on ice. If people could fly there would be events in the air as well. Come to think of it, there could be hang-gliding competitions right now if the Committee would agree to it. Take a look at these snippets from *Record Times* about other events that take place away from the main stadium.

1952 Helsinki

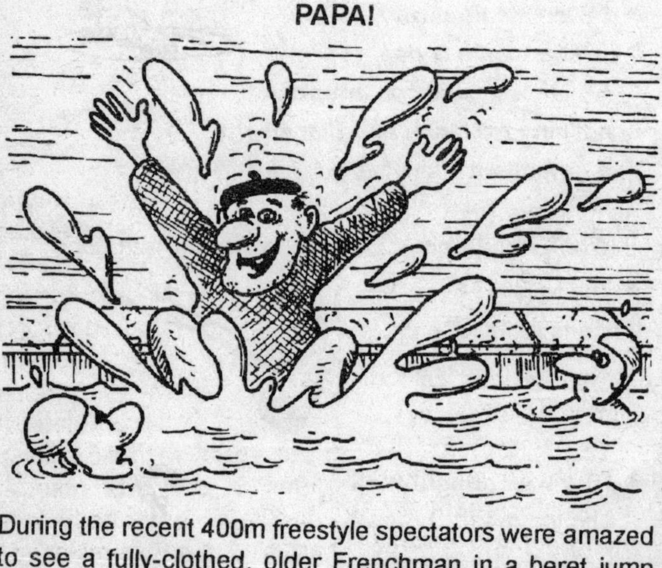

PAPA!

During the recent 400m freestyle spectators were amazed to see a fully-clothed, older Frenchman in a beret jump into the water beside gold-medal-winner Jean Boiteaux of France, just as he touched the wall. Who was this maniac: his coach? an escaped lunatic? No: it was his father!

1928 Amsterdam

SNAP

Lotte Mühe the world record holder has only won bronze in the 200m breastroke. She had to go slow because the straps of her bathing suit snapped - forcing her to stay in the water after the race was over.

1896 Athens

HELP!

French cyclist Flameng has won gold in the 100 kilometre track race by six laps - having already lost time by kindly waiting for a competitor whose bike had broken down to get his bike mended. Flameng rode with the French flag wrapped round his leg.

1964 Lima, Peru

OWN GOAL

328 people have been killed and 500 injured following disgraceful rioting after the qualifying soccer match for the Tokyo Games between Peru and Argentina. It started when two spectators attacked the referee because of his decision to disqualify a Peruvian goal.

1972 Paris

ROAD RAGE

Gold medallist of the 1948 Individual Horse Jumping in London, the Mexican General Humberto Mariles Cortés has died in prison having been arrested for drug-smuggling. General Mariles' career included shooting a fellow motorist with a pistol at traffic lights in 1964 in an early case of road-rage, for which he was arrested, but then released.

Not held since 1908.

Teams of teams

Here are some more events that takes place outside the stadium. Unfortunately there's been a bit of a muddle and everyone's competing in the same place. Some

players have got two heads and some have got three legs. Only one has got both - can you see who it is?

1904 St Louis

GOLD FROM WOOD

George Eyser of America has won gold on the parallel bars and in the long horse vault in the gymnastics competition, as well as silver in the combined event and the pommelled horse. His feat is especially amazing because he has a wooden leg.

1976 Montreal

SHUN'AV DONE IT!

Gymnastics are only for the brave and none are braver than Shun Fujimoto of Japan. Having broken his leg at the knee during the floor exercises, Shun went ahead with the side horse exercises and then the rings. The pain was awful, but it got worse when he landed from the rings - and dislocated his broken knee.

1924 Paris

SCENT OF VICTORY

Jack Beresford of Great Britain has won gold in the single skulls rowing competition on the River Seine. The race took place near a perfumery. The runner-up described the race as having been rowed on a 'river of perfume' in the hot sun.

1976 Montreal

OUR NADIA

Olga Korbut, the 'Munchkin of Munich', who won gold on the balance beam and in the floor exercises at Munich in 1972, has been defeated by tiny Nadia Comaneci of Romania. At a press conference after the tournament Nadia was asked if she would now retire, but she pointed out that she was only fourteen and just wanted to go home

THE HUMAN MACHINE

HOW TO KEEP IT WELL TUNED

- BUT NOT OVER-TUNED

Us ordinary people have quirky bodies: our toes may point in or out a little bit, our arms may be a bit short or a bit long, we may eat too much or too little. That's what makes us interesting. But the body of a top athlete has to work like a perfectly tuned machine if he or she wants to win competitions.

But it's not enough for an athlete to be born with a very good body. They have to work at it. There are lots of people wandering around who *could* have been top athletes, but they chose not to train very hard or spoiled their chances in some other way.

Fit as a slob

The secret of success in sport is *exercise*. Exercise strengthens the muscles and makes the body *fit*. Muscles are powered by food-chemicals in the blood and by oxygen breathed from the air. A fit person is able to get the power they need from food-energy and oygen very quickly, so their muscles can work fast and well. If you puff and pant when you climb the stairs, it's probably because you're *unfit* and your muscles aren't getting their food-energy and oxygen quickly enough - they're gasping for oxygen from the air. In fact you're a bit of a *slob*.

It's not natural to push your body as hard as top athletes have to. People are really designed to *slob* around quite a lot of the time. Athletes have to be *ultra-fit* when they compete in the Olympics. But they also have to look after themselves extra-carefully or they can end up with all kinds of illnesses and injuries. Hippocrates, the Ancient Greek doctor who was the founder of modern medicine, thought that too much fitness was actually dangerous.

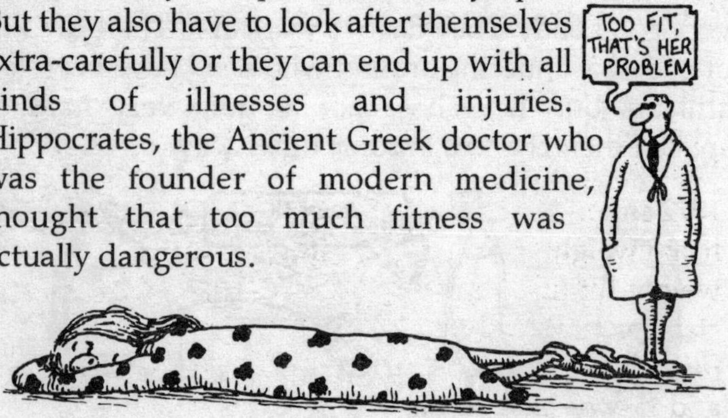

Eat your meat

The food an athlete eats can make a big difference to how he or she performs. Ancient Greek runners ate mainly figs, porridge, meal cakes and cheese, with just a bit of meat and wine from time to time. It was the strongmen such as Milo (see page 84) who ate a lot. He may not have eaten an entire cow in a day, but it seems that he did eat nine kilograms *each* of bread and meat per day - and drank nine litres of wine.

Different sports need different diets. Nowadays, long distance runners eat a lot of energy foods such as bread and spaghetti a little before a race (although when the Finns were doing very well in the 1920s this was put down to their diet of raw, dried fish, hard rye bread and sour milk). But the strongmen (such as Tommy Kono, see page 84) eat lots of meat and eggs to build their muscles. Vassily Alexeyev, 1972 super-heavyweight weight-lifting champion, would breakfast on steak and *twenty-six* fried eggs.

Toughen up!

Athletes use their muscles, heart and lungs in different ways depending on their chosen sport, so they must exercise differently in order to strengthen their bodies in the most useful ways. That's why Ancient Greek runners would practise by running in the sand, boxers would punch a punch-ball filled with sand or millet (a type of grain), and weight-lifters would practise lifting weights - like Milo and the calf. They all toughened up by bathing in rivers and sleeping in the open air.

In 1896, Frenchman Lermusiaux was asked how he was able to train to compete in both the 100m and the 800m. 'It eez simple,' he said in his French accent: 'One day I run a leetle way vairy queek, ze next day I run a long way vairy slow.'

Nowadays a lot is known about how to get the most out of the human body and training has become very scientific. Even back in the 1920s, Paavo Nurmi would train with a stopwatch in his hand. Most athletes now do *interval training*. Interval training involves spurts of hard exercise broken by short distances of jogging. It can be incredibly tough. Emil Zatopek, a famous Czech runner, would sometimes run 400m a *hundred* times in a day, with jogging in between - sixty to seventy kilometres in all.

If it's not hurting it's not working

Emil Zatopek believed that he had to cross the 'pain-barrier' while training, otherwise his body would not become as strong as possible. He once injured himself by training with his wife on his shoulders - even the greatest athletes have their limits!

Drugs

For some athletes, training isn't enough. They take drugs to make themselves perform even better.

There was a time when nobody minded about athletes taking some drugs, but in those days they weren't so widely used and they didn't work so well. Long distance runners might drink pick-me-ups containing large amounts of strychnine sulphate. Strychnine is a deadly poison if not taken with great care. During the St Louis marathon in 1904 Thomas Hicks drank strychnine beaten with egg white with a brandy chaser. He finished in a daze - but he won gold.

Nowadays the rules about drugs are very strict. Even *blood-doping* is looked down on, although it doesn't involve the use of drugs. In blood-doping athletes do their training high up in mountain regions. This increases the number of red oxygen-carrying cells in their blood. Several litres of the enriched blood are then bled off and stored. Shortly before a race the athlete is given an infusion of the stored blood and thus increases his or her 'fitness', by being able to carry more oxygen to their muscles in the recently restored blood.

Don't glug these drugs!

Several types of drug improve the performance of athletes. Of these *anabolic steroids* are the most widely used. Anabolic steroids work a bit like natural male hormones. Male hormones are chemicals which in nature make men 'manly', for instance they give men deep voices and make them grow more body hair and muscle than women. It's the muscles, of course, which some athletes are after - not the hair. After the 1976 Montreal Games, the East German women swimmers were accused of having unusually deep voices and big

muscles. An East German official defended them, replying that the women: 'came to swim, not sing.'

Other drugs which have been taken include *human growth hormone* which is taken from human corpses and increases muscle growth, and *Winstrol-V* which is normally used for injecting into cattle to fatten them before market.

Benoid

Benjamin Johnson won gold in the 100m at Seoul in 1988. He was later stripped of his medal when it was discovered that he'd been taking drugs. He had begun to take steroids in 1981 and since that time he had taken a whole shopping bag of drugs, including steroids, testosterone (a male hormone), human growth hormone, Winstrol-V, and other drugs. His fellow athletes had known for years that Johnson was taking drugs, they called him the 'Benoid ' because of his amazing muscles and yellow-tinged eyes.

 *Benoid* is a mixture of the words *Benjamin* and *android*, meaning a robot.

Testing

Olympic officials do all they can to stop drug-taking. They are now allowed to bust in on an athlete to demand a test at any time, not just before or after a competition. So it's no longer safe for drug-takers to stop taking drugs just before their event and then take other drugs to mask them from the testers, as Johnson tried to do.

Tests usually involve testing an athlete's urine (pee) for the remains of any drugs which may have passed through his or her body. This can cause problems even when an athlete is completely innocent. After winning gold as a middleweight boxer in the 1968 Mexico games, Christopher Finnegan of Great Britain was asked for a sample of urine - but the fact that he was being asked for a sample made him nervous so he couldn't produce one. He drank several glasses of water and four pints of beer, all to no avail. Desperate for a sample, two Olympic drug-testers had to follow him wherever he went, in case he was holding back so as to avoid the test. He finally went to the toilet at 1.40

am in a restaurant. Fortunately, the test was negative.

It's all in the mind

Apart from hard training and the right food there's one other thing that can help athletes to win, and that's how they prepare their minds for the strain of competing in front of millions of people. It's a serious problem. Bad nerves can make all the difference between a gold medal and no medal at all. To overcome the nerves of his American gymnasts, one trainer told them to imagine that they were in the Olympic finals and that their team was neck-and-neck with the Chinese. They had to try to imagine this situation every day for several minutes.

Lo and behold, during the 1984 Games in Los Angeles, gymnast Peter Vidmar found himself up against the Chinese and with equal points between the two teams! His training worked. He'd imagined the situation so many times before that he didn't feel nervous - and he and his team went on to win gold.

Even during the Games an athlete's state of mind can change, making a difference to how he or she performs. Fifteen miles into the 1952 marathon Emil Zatopek turned to the British favourite, James Peters, and said: 'Excuse me, I haven't run a marathon before, but don't you think we ought to go a little faster?' Peters was horrified - wasn't Zatopek tired at all? From then on Zatopek had the advantage. He won (although his legs were so sore that he couldn't walk for a week afterwards).

Only dreaming

When she went to sleep the night before the final of the women's 100m freestyle swimming at the 1956 Melbourne Games, Dawn Fraser was already very nervous about the next day's race. That night she dreamt that her feet were stuck to the starting block with honey and when at last she did manage to dive into the pool, she dreamt that the pool was full of spaghetti. She woke up sweating and flailing her arms as if drowning in a sea of spaghetti. Fortunately she managed to get over her nightmare - and win gold.

ARE YOU AN OLYMPICS EXPERT?

Now that you've read this far, you've got a *sporting* chance of doing this quiz.

(Answers on page 123.)

1 What is interval training?

a Spurts of hard exercise broken by intervals of jogging

b Spurts of hard exercise broken by short snoozes

c Training on alternate days

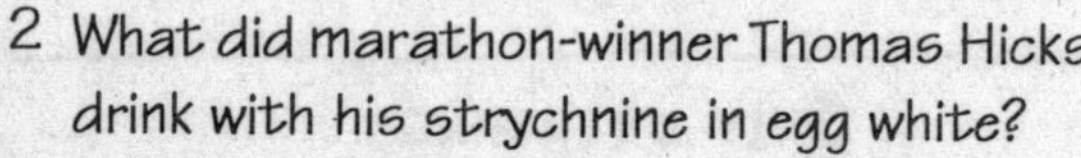

2 What did marathon-winner Thomas Hicks drink with his strychnine in egg white?

a A whisky chaser

b A brandy chaser

c Pure spring water

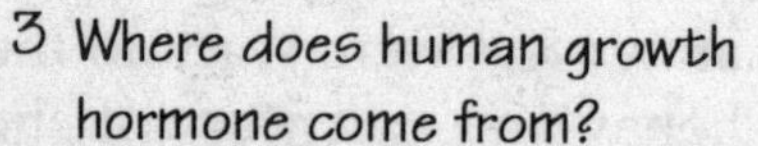

3 Where does human growth hormone come from?

a Live hormone-donors

b Human corpses

c Genetically engineered mice

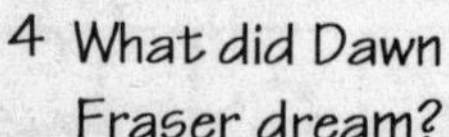

4 What did Dawn Fraser dream?

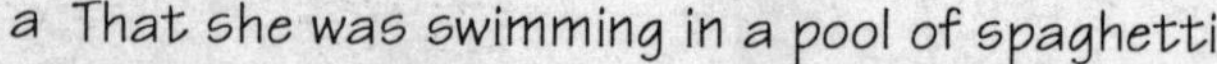

a That she was swimming in a pool of spaghetti

b That she had to eat a bowl of spaghetti

c That she was swimming in a pool of honey

GALLERY OF GREATS

A CHOICE OF CHAMPIONS

Are you hung up on sport? Step into this picture gallery and take a look at some of the all-time Olympic greats who have been hung up on its walls.

JIM THORPE

(1888-1953)

James F. Thorpe was the star athlete of the fifth Olympics in Stockholm in 1912, winning the pentathlon and the decathlon. Thorpe was an interesting mixture: he was part Irish, part Sac, Fox, Potawatomie and Kickapoo native American, and part French. He never trained too much and won competitions by sheer, natural talent. He was a bit of a superman: apart from athletics he was also brilliant at baseball and American football and even won a ballroom dancing championship when he was a student.

When congratulated by King Gustav of Sweden after the Stockholm Games, Thorpe thanked him with the immortal words: 'Thanks, King.' But Thorpe had his enemies. The Amateur Athletic Union of America discovered that he had once been paid a few dollars for playing baseball. They declared that he was a professional (see page 37), and not a proper amateur. They stripped him of all his medals. For much of the rest of his life he had to scrape a living doing various odd jobs: he worked as a sailor and a bouncer, and even as an Indian chief in Hollywood films.

History has been kinder to Jim Thorpe than the Amateur Athletic Union. When he died in 1953, the small town of Mauch Chunk in Pennsylvania changed its name to *James Thorpe Town* in his honour. His monument there reads: 'Sir, you are the greatest athlete in the world!'

PAAVO NURMI

(1897-1973) - the Flying Finn

Paavo Nurmi was the king of long distance running in the 1920s. He competed in the 1920 Antwerp Games and in all games up to Los Angeles 1932. That was when, like Jim Thorpe before him, Paavo was accused of not being a true amateur and was banned from the Olympics (this slur was removed twenty-four years later when he was asked to carry the torch at the 1956 Helsinki Games).

Paavo didn't smile much, he acted like a machine for running. People loved him for his victories and hated him for his unsmiling face - he was once voted the most popular Finn and the most unpopular Finn at the same time in the same opinion poll! Once on the track, he used to ignore his fellow competitors and would decide when to increase his speed by looking at his stopwatch. That was his secret - he raced against the clock and against himself. In all, he won nine gold medals, three of silver and bronze and set twenty-nine world records during his career.

Fanny (Francina) Blankers-Koen

(1918 -) - the Flying Dutch Housewife

Fanny was already thirty by the time of the 1948 London Games. She had been in the 1936 Games when she was eighteen but since then the War had stopped any further games. Most people thought she was too old to do very well.

How wrong they were! She won gold in the 100m, the 200m, the 80m hurdle and the 100m relay. She could have won gold in the long jump too if she'd bothered to enter it - the winning long jump was a full fifty centimetres short of her world record.

On her return to Amsterdam she was driven through the streets in triumph in a carriage drawn by four grey horses. Her neighbours gave her a bike: 'So she wouldn't have to run so much'.

Sonja Henie

(1912-69)

Sonja Henie was the daughter of a Norwegian fur trader. She ruled the world of figure skating during the 1930s, winning gold at the 1928, 1932 and 1936 Winter Olympics, as well as *1,473* other cups and trophies. By 1936 she was so popular that police were needed to protect her from the crowds of her supporters. It was in that year she at last turned professional and later became a film star, starring in twelve films. She was also a brilliant businesswoman. When she died she left forty-seven million dollars - at least half a billion at today's value.

EMIL ZÁTOPEK

(1922-) - the Czech Steam Engine

Emil was a soldier in the Czech army. He was a man of iron. He probably trained harder than any athlete had ever trained before. When on sentry duty he would run on the spot for hours on end. In winter, in army boots, he would run through the snow-clad Czech forests for mile after mile with a strange, long, leaping stride so as to strengthen his legs still further.

Emil was a friendly, talkative person, but you would never have guessed it from watching him run. From the legs up he looked like he was in agony - his head lolled, his face was screwed up, his tongue hung out, he looked alarmingly as if he might have a heart attack at any moment. But although he had zero style, he knew how to win races. He won four gold medals, set eighteen world records and dominated long distance running from his first Olympic triumph at the 1948 London Games until Helsinki 1956.

Jean-Claude Killy

(1944-)

Frenchman Jean-Claude was one of the greatest winter champions of all time. He always loved danger. As a young man he once dropped his trousers during a ski jump, landing in his long johns, which sounds like a pretty mad thing to do and must also be quite dangerous. He won three gold medals at the 1968 Grenoble Games but turned professional immediately afterwards in order to make money advertising ski equipment.

Mark Spitz

(1950-)

Mark Spitz won the most gold medals ever won in a single Olympic Games - seven of them, at the 1972 Münich Games. Everyone else might just as well have stayed at home. His father Arnold was a bit of an Ancient Greek and had always told him: 'Swimming isn't everything, winning is.' Which is a long way from Baron Pierre de Coubertin's original Olympic ideal - but worked for Spitz.

Sebastian Coe

(1956-)

Together with his rival and fellow British athlete Steve Ovett, Sebastian Coe is one of the greatest British runners of all time. At the 1980 Moscow Games Sebastian Coe won gold at Ovett's best distance, the 1,500m and Steve Ovett won gold at Sebastian's best distance, the 800m.

Carl Lewis

(1961 -)

Carl was small and shy as a little child, but when he was fifteen he grew so fast that he shot up like a rocket - so fast that he had to wear crutches for three weeks because his body wasn't ready to support the extra height.

He grew into one of the greatest running machines of all time, winning gold in the 1984 Los Angeles 100m and shattering world records like plates in a Greek restaurant. He won gold again in Seoul in 1988 - after Ben Johnson had been stripped of gold for taking drugs (see page 106).

RACES IN SPACE

WHAT THE FUTURE HOLDS

TEN BACK-SOMERSAULTS AND A FLIP

Heroes come and heroes go, but the Olympics keep on growing. They're like a sprinter on steroids. *Three billion people* are expected to tune in to the 2000 Sydney Olympics. That's more than the total population of the world in 1950, just fifty years before.

And there are still hundreds of sports queuing up to join the Games. Small wonder - if sports become 'Olympic' sports, they get seen more on television, so more people play them. It's not just a question of established sports like cricket or golf which are no longer included in the Olympics, new sports are being invented all the time. Snow-boarding or paragliding could be just the start, soon we could be watching weightless gymnasts performing in space stadiums! (Although one thing we'll probably never see is weightless weight-lifting!)

Where will it all end? The world's population is growing larger and larger, and soon there might even be as many television sets as people. Most of those sets will be switched on to the Olympics for at least some of the time that future Games are being held. The more people that watch, the more money the Games will make. Money that, among other things, will be spent on building ever larger stadiums for more and more sports and competitors - so that even *more* people will either tune in or or take part.

GOLD!

The Games may have grown but de Coubertin's Olympic dream lives on. Athletes will still be welcomed whether they're black or white, big or small.

And for the athletes, despite the huge crowds and the television cameras, one thing hasn't really changed since the Ancient Greeks ran naked in the sun-baked stadium at Ancient Olympia. There'll still be nothing to compare with winning in competition against their fellow athletes - nothing like gold to tell them they're the best there is.

SYDNEY 2000

SPORTS ROUND-UP

Time: September 13 - October 1, 2000
Place: Sydney, Australia
Number of sports: 28 (counting athletics as one)
New Olympic sports: Taekwondo, trampolining discipline, canoe slalom, the triathlon and women's water polo.

1. Aquatics (swimming, water polo, diving and synchronised swimming)

2. Archery

3. Athletics (track and field)

4. Badminton

5. Baseball

7. Boxing

6. Basketball

8. Canoe/Kayak (sprint and slalom)

9. Cycling (track, road and mountain bike)

10. Equestrian (jumping, dressage , and three-day event)

11. Fencing (foil, épée, sabre)

Dressage means training a horse to high levels of obedience.

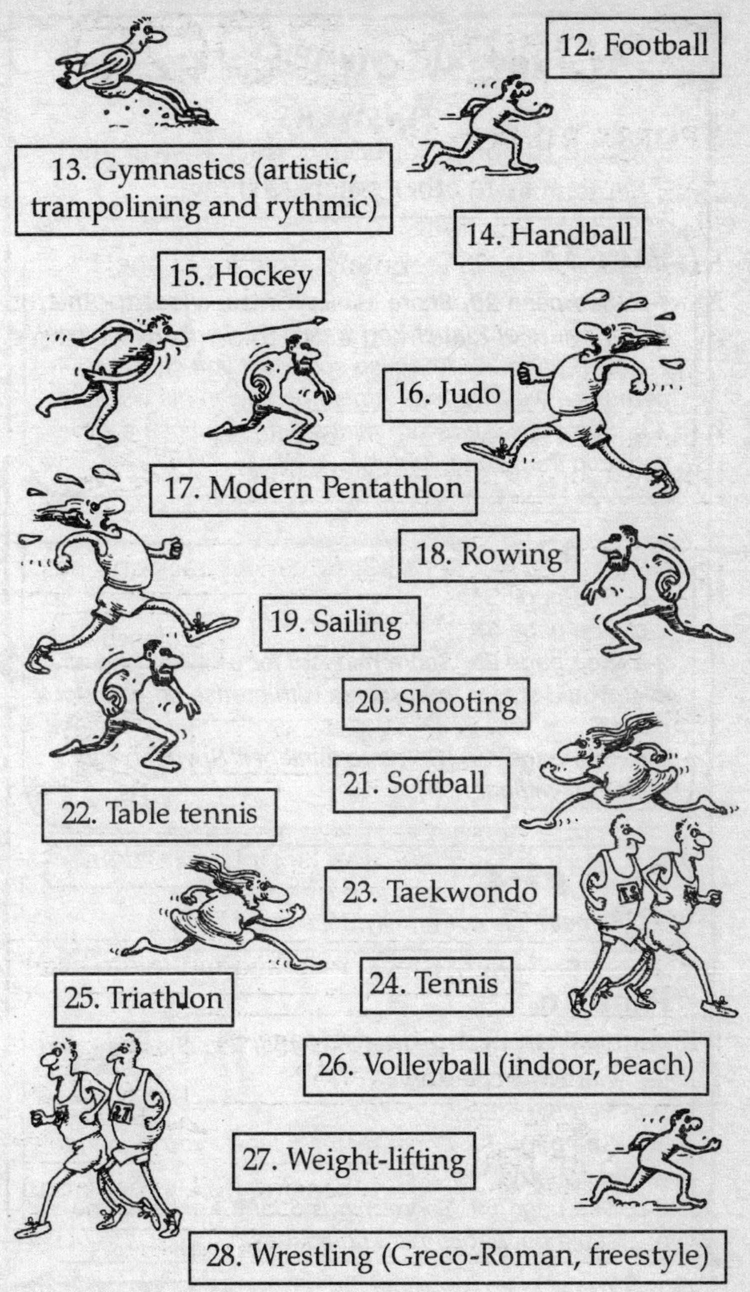
12. Football
13. Gymnastics (artistic, trampolining and rythmic)
14. Handball
15. Hockey
16. Judo
17. Modern Pentathlon
18. Rowing
19. Sailing
20. Shooting
21. Softball
22. Table tennis
23. Taekwondo
24. Tennis
25. Triathlon
26. Volleyball (indoor, beach)
27. Weight-lifting
28. Wrestling (Greco-Roman, freestyle)

Are you an Olympics expert? Answers

Score 10 points for each correct answer and score other points as shown.

Page 33

1-b. See page 29. Score minus 5 if you chose c *- The Axe Masters of Planet Zog wasn't de Coubertin's taste!*
2-c. See page 25. And also score 5 if you chose a *- perhaps it was Thomas Arnold he saw in his vision!*
3-c. See page 31. Score minus 5 if you chose a *- you're in the wrong century!*

Page 42

1-b. See page 35.
2-c. See page 35.
3-a. See page 39. Score minus 5 for c *- what kind of idiot would smear themselves with grease so as to look good?*
4-b. See page 40. (Come to think of it Spyridon was better off without her!)

Pages 62-3

3,000 metres is not an Olympic race.

Page 76

1-b. See page 64. Score minus 10 if you chose a *- and get your brain checked!*
2-a. See page 66.
3-b. See page 71. Score minus 5 for c *- you're in the wrong country!*
4-c. See page 69. Score minus 5 for b *- although no one could be that stupid - could they?!*

Page 93

1-b. See page 79. Score minus 5 if you chose a *- ancient Greek athletes competed naked.*
2-a. See page 84. Score minus 5 for c *- for obvious reasons!*
3-c. See page 87.
4-c. See page 89. Score minus 5 if you chose a *or* b*, whoever heard of an Olympic champion being descended from an ice giant?*

Page 110

1-a. See page 103. Score minus 5 for b - you'll never become an athlete if you break off training for snoozes.
2-b. See page 104. Score 5 for c. It's wrong - but it was worth a try!
3-b. See page 106.
4-a. See page 109.

Grand total

150-200	You are seriously expert, but you spend too much time reading books - go out and get some exercise!
100-150	Perfect - you are clever, well-adjusted and probably athletic.
50-100	Oh dear! Read this book again - and this time read it properly.
less than 50	Sad, very sad! That was hopeless. Give up reading and take up sport - it's your only chance.

INDEX

Now Read On

If you want to know more about the Olympics, see if your local library or bookshop has either of these books.

OLYMPICS FACTS AND FEATS
By Stan Greenberg (Guiness Publishing 1996) Bewilder your friends with detailed data. This book lists all the medallists from the beginning of the modern Olympics and gives a complete list of Olympic records at the date of publication. A must for every sports fan.

THE COMPLETE BOOK OF THE OLYMPICS
By David Wallechinsky (Aurum Press 1992) This really is the ultimate Olympics handbook. It's what every sports journalist would carry in his or her back pocket - if the pocket were big enough! What David Wallechinsky doesn't know about the Olympics is probably not worth knowing about. Read this book and die knowlegeable!

About the Author

Bob Fowke is a well-known author of children's information books. Writing under various pen names and with various friends and colleagues, he has created many unusual and entertaining works on all manner of subjects.

There's always more to his books than meets the eye - check out the index at the back of this one!

OTHER BOOKS IN THIS SERIES

ANCIENT EGYPTIANS by David Jay. They used monkeys to arrest burglars!

ANCIENT GREEKS by Bob Fowke. They thought and they fought.

ROMANS IN BRITAIN by Bob Fowke. From slaves to emperors - and things in between.

ANGLO-SAXONS by Bob Fowke. There's blood on your boar-crests, brothers!

VIKINGS by Bob Fowke. Fancy a bowl of blood soup before bedtime?

HENRY VIII, HIS FRIENDS AND RELATIONS by Fred Finney. Too much meat, not enough toilets!

ELIZABETH I, HER FRIENDS AND RELATIONS by Bob Fowke. When men wore their knickers outside their tights ...

SHAKESPEARE by Anita Ganeri. What the brilliant bard and his mad mates were really like.

QUEEN VICTORIA, HER FRIENDS AND RELATIONS by Fred Finney. Watch out for the dumpy little lady in black.

WORLD WAR II by Bob Fowke. Who won the War, and why men didn't have jacket pockets.

Plus !..
ART by Catherine Charley
LIVING THINGS by Bob Fowke
MUSIC by Nicola Barber
PIRATES OF THE PAST by Jim Hatfield
PLANET EARTH by Bob Fowke
SCIENCE by Bob Fowke
VILLAINS THROUGH THE AGES by Jim Hatfield